M000229255

HOW TO BE A
GREAT
REAL ESTATE
AGENT

*The Principles of
Client-Oriented Real Estate
(CORE)*

HOW TO BE A
GREAT
REAL ESTATE
AGENT

*The Principles of
Client-Oriented Real Estate
(CORE)*

JOE RAND

ILLUSTRATIONS BY NATE FAKES

Copyright © 2019 by Joe Rand

All rights reserved. This book or any portion thereof may not be reproduced or used in any manner whatsoever without the express written permission of the publisher except for the use of brief quotations in a book review.

ISBN 978-1-947635-16-6 (Paperback Edition)

Printed in the United States of America

First Printing January 2019

Published by Hart Place Publishing

hartplacebooks.com

info@hartplacebooks.com

Contents

1   Author's Preface:
     Be Great at Your Job

15   **Introduction**

17   The CORE Formula

31   **Part One: Client Development**

33   Chapter 1
     Who's Your Agent?

43   Chapter 2
     The Sphere of Support:
     They're All Clients

55   Chapter 3
     The Top 100 Referral System:
     Not All Heroes Wear a Cape

73   Chapter 4
     From Old to SOLD:
     The Bottle of Wine

95   Part One Conclusion:
     Be Great at Your Job

99   **Part Two: Client Conversion**

101 Chapter 5
     The Consultative Presentation

109 Chapter 6
     The Needs Consultation:
     It's Not About You

119   Chapter 7
      The Project Plan:
      The CORE Services

135   Chapter 8
      The Collaborative Pricing Process:
      Damn, Real Estate Agents!

147   Chapter 9
      The Buyer Consultation:
      No, We Didn't Forget...

155   Part Two Conclusion:
      Be Great at Your Job

157   **Part Three: Client Management**

159   Chapter 10
      What People Need:
      Getting to Delight

167   Chapter 11
      Creative Systems:
      The "Clean Windows" Protocols

177   Chapter 12
      Executing Well:
      The "No Brown M&Ms" Action Plans

185   Chapter 13
      The Ten Elements of
      Great Client Experiences

207   Part Three Conclusion:
      Be Great at Your Job

211   **Conclusion**

213   Be Great at Your Job

217   **Afterword: Where Do We Go From Here?**

221   **Acknowledgements**

Author's Preface:
Be Great at Your Job

BE GREAT AT YOUR JOB.

Be great at your job of helping people sell homes.

Be great at your job of helping people buy homes.

Be great at your job of helping people even when they're not buying or selling homes.

Just be great at your job.

Lesson One: The Seller Agents

I was an overpriced seller.

At long last, I can admit that. Whew! It actually feels pretty good to get that off my chest.

We should have some sort of support group for sellers like me. Big room down in the local church basement, filled with people who can't sell their homes.

"I'm Joe, and I'm a price-aholic."

"Hi Joe!"

So go ahead, roll your eyes. Another overpriced seller, and one that should have definitely known better. After all, for almost 20 years, I had been one of the managing brokers for my family's real estate brokerage in New York and New Jersey, one of the biggest family-owned companies in the country. In fact, for most of that time, I'd been in charge of agent education, and over the years I'd taught thousands of agents how to persuade sellers to price their homes to the market, and how to keep them from making the big mistake of, you know, overpricing their home.

But I was like every other seller. I wanted what every seller wants and said what every seller said and what every broker hates to hear:

Let's test the market.

I'm not in any hurry to sell.

I can always come down later.

It only takes ONE buyer!

Man, I was a nightmare. But luckily for me, I had two really great agents. I could have just listed it myself, of course, or listed it with another one of the innumerable members of the Rand family who are all licensed real estate professionals: my mother, my wife, my three brothers, a few cousins, and maybe a few distant relatives I'm not even aware of.

But to paraphrase the old adage, "a REALTOR who represents himself has a big dummy for a client."

(Editor's note: not the actual adage).

So I hired two agents the most meritocratic way I could think of: Margo, the top-producing agent at my company, and Donna, the top agent at the local office. They're both great, they've both been with my firm for a long time, and I like and respect both of them.

And they did a terrific job. They created a beautiful marketing plan: alluring photos, engaging copy, a hardcover coffee table photo book, a 3D walkthrough, all really impressive stuff. They also guided me through the process of staging my home, which was not easy given that I had two kids under the age of three living with me.

Plus, I'm a slob.

And a packrat.

So like I said, not easy.

The only thing they couldn't do was get me to price my home where they suggested. Now, in my defense, or perhaps to explain my self-rationalization, my home was not easy to comp. It had a bit of that "best house on the block" problem: a 4,500 square foot penthouse condo with panoramic views of the Hudson River that was twice the size of any other unit in the building (or the county), with a higher level of amenities than anything else in the area. So despite their advice, I went high, and they reluctantly agreed to indulge me.

And for a while, nothing happened. Lots of activity and show-ings, but no offers. So after a few months of that, they gave me a call and suggested that we meet:

Hey Joe, let's sit down to, you know, discuss the marketing...

Uh-oh, I knew what that meant! Heck, for 20 years I'd taught agents how to approach the "price improvement" meeting with an overpriced seller.

So I laughed:

Please, I know that line. I've TAUGHT that line. You don't want to talk about the marketing, you want to beat me up on price!

They protested:

No, No, No! We just want to talk about how the marketing is going.

So we set up an appointment.

And they sat down.

And then they started beating me up on price.

But, like I said, they are really great agents. They didn't just tell me the obvious, that we needed to reduce because we hadn't gotten any offers yet. Instead, they showed me. Specifically, they showed me what had happened to the buyers who had seen my condo, following up with all the agents and pulling the listings those buyers had ultimately purchased instead.

And they opened my eyes. Yes, my condo was tough to comp, but after six months on the market we now had real-life behavioral feedback showing us what our potential buyers had decided to purchase instead. And what we found was that they were not necessarily getting condos in the area, as we had expected. Instead, they were buying houses with small lots and limited maintenance, particularly in a nearby upscale area called Tweed Boulevard, which was on a cliff facing the Hudson with similar views to mine. Or they were looking outside the area, in higher-end markets across the river in Westchester.

The point was, we now had comps, and those comps were telling me one thing: we were overpriced. I was losing credible buyers to lower-priced properties in the same market, or higher-priced properties in higher-end markets. So after some hemming and hawing, I agreed to make a pretty sizable reduction to bring our listing in line with what the market was telling us.

But they weren't done. They also had a suggestion on the staging. Now, I'd already moved out a lot of stuff, enough to fill a 20'x20' storage unit from top to bottom. But I was still living in the condo with my wife and two young kids. And that was a problem.

So they told me I should move out! Summer was coming, and we had a beach house about an hour away. They suggested we spend a month or so there and do another round of de-cluttering to get rid of all the kid stuff. They told me that would make a significant difference for the kind of buyers we were looking for, most of whom were older couples looking for a trophy property who couldn't envision themselves living in a condo with kids' toys in every corner.

They convinced me again. We moved out.

Within about a week of that meeting, my family had moved to the Jersey Shore, cleared out all the kid junk (and more of our stuff), and we'd reduced the price significantly.

We were in contract two weeks later.

Agents who are great at their jobs get their listings sold.

Lesson Two: The Buyer Agent

Here's another story, this time about an angry phone call I got one day from a lawyer representing a local condo development board.

I get those types of calls from time to time. I'm also the attorney for my company, which is the worst part of my job because I have to deal with complaints. And lawyers. And complaints from lawyers. Like I said, the worst.

I never get happy calls. No one ever calls the attorney for a real estate brokerage to say how happy they are. No, I only get the call if the person can't be satisfied talking to, in order: the agent, or their manager, or their regional director, or any of the other Rands. Only the angriest of the angry, the curdled cream of that dreadful crop, end up in my inbox.

This was one of those angry calls. It seems that one of my agents, a woman we'll call Stacy, had been going door-to-door in the condo complex soliciting owners for a listing, which was a violation of association rules. I heard out the lawyer and promised to look into it.

So I gave her a call to find out what happened and to let her know that she needed to comply with the board rules. I figured that she had just gotten a little overly exuberant with her prospecting, particularly looking for listings in what, at the time, was a sizzling market with low inventory.

But that wasn't quite it. Turns out that she was representing a pair of first-time home buyers with a baby on the way who were desperate to buy something, and who were devastated that they had just missed out on their third bidding war. This condo development was perfect for them, but none of the units were on the market. So Stacy had promised them that she would approach all the homeowners in the complex and find out whether any of them were interested in selling sometime soon with the hopes of getting her buyers in there. That's why she was going door-to-door.

Now, that whole "My buyers missed out!" approach is of course one of those classic real estate prospecting campaigns, popularized most recently by my friend and colleague, the brilliant Tom Ferry: blanket a neighborhood with solicitations that you have real buyers trying to move in and see if you can shake out a new listing.

Some agents, of course, will send out the mailing as a gimmick without actually having a new buyer. But in this case, Stacy had a buyer and she wasn't trying to score a new listing. She was literally just trying to find her clients a place to live by fishing upstream of the market.

Nevertheless, I had to break it to her that she couldn't go door-to-door in the complex, since the board had rules against those types of solicitations. But I was honestly impressed with her dedication to helping her buyers, so I made a suggestion: contact the condo board president, apologize and explain the situation, and offer to host a seminar in the common room about what was happening with the local market. I told her I'd help her put together a package of material on local values and contribute toward getting an urn of coffee and some treats.

She was a pretty persuasive and persistent agent, so she managed to get the board to agree to hold the event. A few weeks later, she got about 20 homeowners to come down for an hour of conversation about the market.

But she didn't get a listing out of it.

She got three.

And her buyers bought one of them.

Agents who are great at their jobs find their buyers homes.

Lesson Three: The Rock Salt

It was just a bag of rock salt. A $10 bag of rock salt, sitting on the front stoop, tied up with a ribbon stapled to a simple "thank you" note.

And it was one of the best things Bill—a real estate agent from upstate New York—ever did for a client.

Bill was just doing a basic "pop-by," part of the coaching program he followed with Brian Buffini. Brian is an excellent real estate coach who teaches agents how to build a referral business by cultivating a database of clients through a campaign involving monthly items of value, regular phone calls, personal notes, and what he calls "pop-bys"—a quick visit with a top referral client to bring them a small but meaningful gift, a way of thanking them for their support and building the relationship.

Bill's approach to the pop-by was smart. He would keep an eye out for the first snowfall of the year and, when it approached, he would go out to a home improvement store and buy a bunch of 10-pound bags of rock salt. He'd write a personal note (a Buffini mandate!), staple it to a ribbon, and tie it to the bag. Then he'd load it all in his truck and deliver a bag to each of his best referral clients.

A clever idea. In just a few hours, for not a lot of money, he would make a thoughtful gesture for his best referral clients. A nice little service for the people who supported him.

Bill did this every year, and he always got a bunch of calls from his clients thanking him for the gift. But one year he got a very special call from one of his best referral clients. It went something like this:

Hey, I just wanted to thank you for dropping off the rock salt. The thing is, my wife and I were at the doctor's office, because she's been going through some health issues. And it wasn't a great visit, so we were a little upset as we were driving home. That's when we saw that it was starting to snow, and I realized that I'd forgotten to get any rock salt.

So here I was, bringing my wife back from the doctor, and I realized I'd have to drop her off and leave her alone at the house while I ran out to the hardware store. She understood but I still felt like I was letting her down.

Then, as I pulled into the driveway, we saw the bag of rock salt by the front door. We both started to laugh. And then we both started to cry.

I just wanted you to know, it meant a lot to us in that moment. Thank you.

How wonderful is that? No, seriously, how wonderful is that? Can you imagine having the opportunity to touch someone's life like that in such a meaningful way? That's what it's all about, isn't it?

I just love that story. I love how that agent created such a moving experience with something as simple as a bag of rock salt. He didn't spend a lot of money or invest a lot of time. He just made a modest gesture, providing a thoughtful service to the people he cared about, those who supported his business. He could never have anticipated the kind of meaningful impact that gift would make, but by taking that sort of approach to the people in his life, he put himself in the position to create a memorable client experience.

Can you imagine how many times that client has told that story, about how his real estate agent dropped off a bag of rock salt? I mean, I wasn't even there, and I've told the story a hundred times. And now I've written about it!

Agents who are great at their jobs make differences in the lives of people who aren't even selling or buying a home.

Be Great at Your Job

Successful real estate agents are great at their jobs. They're great at helping people sell homes. They're great at helping people buy homes. They're even great at helping people who aren't buying or selling a home at all.

Margo and Donna, Stacy, and Bill all had one thing in common: they were great at their jobs. Margo and Donna found the right way to help me make an enlightened decision on price. Stacy went above-and-beyond to try to find her desperate buyers a home. Bill took it upon himself to make sure his referral clients were prepared for the first snow of winter.

Even better, because they were great at their jobs, they succeeded. Margo and Donna sold a listing. Stacy not only found her buyers a home, but got a couple of extra listings out of her initiative. Bill cemented a relationship that assuredly brought him a myriad of personal referrals for years and years.

Doesn't that make sense? I mean, wouldn't you think that being great at your job would be the key to being successful? Just look around you. Most successful professionals are great at their jobs. They're great at being doctors, or lawyers, or architects, or plumbers, or mechanics, or electricians, or hair stylists, or whatever. Put it this way: do you know any really terrific mechanics or doctors or hair stylists who are starving?

So why should things be different in the real estate industry? Why do we have this conception that to be a successful real estate agent, you just need to be good at sales?

- Why do we recruit people when we think that they have the "gift of gab," rather than hire for client service skills?

- Why do we then train those agents almost exclusively on how to prospect for leads, rather than educating them about how to help people buy and sell homes?

- And why do we then send them out of the field armed entirely with tools and systems to help them generate and close leads, rather than assist their clients through a complicated and difficult real estate transaction?

Now, let me be clear that sales skills and tools are absolutely crucial to real estate success. Any professional responsible for generating her own business needs to develop the ability to cultivate clients. Back when I was a young associate working at Debevoise & Plimpton, a big law firm in Manhattan, for example, my supervising partners encouraged me to build relationships with corporate executives who might refer us legal work. We even had firm-wide seminars on networking and pitching. Everyone understood that "if you want to make partner, you need to make rain."

But Debevoise understood the importance of maintaining a balance. Yes, business generation was crucial. But so was making sure we did a great job taking care of the legal needs of those clients we generated. They hired us for our legal abilities, trained us as lawyers, gave us the support to provide outstanding services to our clients, and only *then* did they teach us how to build our business.

That's the balance we've lost in the real estate industry. Yes, of course agents need the skills and tools to canvass for business, follow up with leads, convert appointments, and maintain relationships. But they also have the responsibility to actually provide the real estate services that they're selling: counseling, pricing, staging, marketing, screening, showing, negotiating, communication, and everything else they do to manage the transactional process from consultation to contract to closing.

Essentially, real estate agents have two very difficult and demanding jobs: (1) salesperson, and (2) service professional. The problem is that the real estate industry provides them with the training, tools, and systems to manage only one of them. In my book *Disruptors, Discounters, and Doubters*, I call this the "Original Sin" of the real estate industry: this misconception that real estate agents are only salespeople, leading to a sales-exclusive mindset that dominates the way we hire, train, and support them.

Indeed, for years I've heard trainer after trainer hector real estate agents that their job isn't to help people buy and sell houses. No, their job is to prospect! Make cold calls! Set appointments! Learn 23 different ways to move in for the close! Sales Sales Sales!

But this kind of approach is simply not sustainable for long-term success. Yes, traditional prospecting does generate business, at least in the short term. If you make hours and hours of calls every day to people asking them when they plan on moving, you'll get leads out of it. Absolutely!

Most agents, though, can't keep up a hardcore campaign of cold-call prospecting for very long. They'll go to a seminar, get all fired up about how simple it is to just sit down and plow through until they get an appointment, and then they'll try to actually do it for a few days. Or a few hours. Or, like, 30 minutes. They just can't keep it up, because it's a brutal way to live.

Moreover, even if you can bear to grind through those traditional prospecting campaigns, you still need to develop the skills to take care of all those leads you generate. Helping people buy and sell homes is a demanding and difficult job, and if you're not good at it, you won't build a sustainable career. Your overpriced, poorly marketed listings won't sell. Your mishandled buyers will go work with someone else. Your deals will fall apart. And your unhappy former clients will spread the word that you can't be trusted.

In other words, it's really hard to build a successful real estate career without being really good at your actual job of helping people buy and sell real estate. And, if anything, it's going to get even harder, because clients are more empowered than ever before, and are finally becoming more selective about choosing an agent to work with.

That's something new. For too long, consumers were not that choosy about their real estate agent. They would walk into an office and take the up-person or click a button on a website and work with whoever called them back, or just take whichever agent happened to be at the right open house at the right time. They'd hire the agent who happened to call them out of the blue to find out when they planned on moving. Or they would work with their brother-in-law, or friend, or neighbor, or that nice person from the bridge club, regardless of whether those agents were full-time or part-time, successful or starving, or any good at their job.

Traditionally, most clients didn't choose their agent. Their agent chose them.

And that lack of selectivity kept a lot of mediocre brokers and agents in the business. They weren't good at their jobs, but they could still scratch out a few deals a year by selling their best friend a house, or by being in the right place at the right time when a ready buyer clicked on "find out more" on their company website.

But that's changing. In a culture where people increasingly won't buy a book without reading the reviews on Amazon, or eat at a restaurant without checking out Yelp, consumers are starting to become more selective about their real estate agents. They're reading the online reviews. They're reviewing performance analytics. They're checking references. They're asking their friends. Clients will increasingly be rewarding the agents who are great at their jobs – and avoiding the ones who are not.

So in this new era, where clients are more in control than ever, we can't do things the ways we've always done them. We need to be great at our jobs.

Introducing Client-Oriented Real Estate

That's why I created the program I call "Client-Oriented Real Estate," or "CORE," which flips the mindset from thinking about ourselves to thinking about our clients. Specifically, CORE teaches agents how to become successful by expanding their conception both about what their clients need and the services they can provide to satisfy those needs.

For too long, the industry has been agent-oriented or broker-oriented, obsessing about what we need: leads, listings, sales, the next commission check. But that mindset is simply not sustainable in an era where consumers are more empowered and demanding than ever before. Instead, we need to start focusing on what our clients need from us. We can't be industry-oriented. We can't be sales-oriented. We have to be client-oriented.

Think about how Margo and Donna approached convincing me to make a price adjustment on my listing: they knew what I needed even when I didn't. Even better, they figured out a smart way to bring me to the light. Many agents would have simply told me that the condo was overpriced, taking it as self-evident from the fact that it hadn't sold. But Margo and Donna went the extra step of tracking down the people who'd come for showings and finding out what they had bought. That was data I didn't have before and it made the difference. They knew that I didn't need to be badgered about how my listing was overpriced. Instead, I needed to see how I'd missed out on serious buyers who had gone on to other opportunities.

Similarly, Stacy thought expansively about what her buyers needed: not just a new listing in that development—where they'd risk losing yet another bidding war—but an opportunity to find a condo that wasn't even on the market yet. And then she was creative in trying to satisfy that need. She didn't just send a "my buyer missed out!" mailing to the development, she actually went door to door and, when she got in trouble for doing that, she held an event onsite to attract potential sellers.

And Bill took this approach to an entirely new level. He wasn't even working with someone buying or selling a home. Rather, he expanded his entire conception of what the people in his life needed and the kinds of services that he could provide to them. Technically, of course, a real estate agent isn't responsible for buying people rock salt for the season's first snowfall. But Bill took a broader view of what he could do for his top referral sources: if they needed rock salt, he was going to get them some rock salt.

Why did they all succeed? Because they thought expansively about what their clients needed and creatively about how to get it for them. They were client-oriented, not agent-oriented.

CORE comes from the experiences I've had working with thousands of agents over the past 20 years. When I started teaching in the real estate industry, I was a real estate broker, not an independent trainer or coach. I didn't make money by selling books, or seminars, or coaching. I only made money when my agents made money. So I didn't have the luxury of teaching a niche program ("follow my foolproof FSBO campaign!") that would only work for a small group of agents. And I didn't have any interest in building an army of fearless but hapless prospecting machines who burned every client they touched, undermining my brand and injuring my business in the long run. I needed a program that would work to help my agents—all my agents—generate business.

That's when I started paying more attention to what the top agents in my market were doing. What made them successful? What did they have in common? It wasn't easy to figure out. They didn't look the same, they didn't talk the same, they didn't work the same. Some were archetypical salespeople: charming, gregarious, charismatic, with the natural ability to win clients over. But others were quiet and reserved, diligent technicians who defied easy stereotyping.

And I found that very few of them were doing what I thought of as hardcore prospecting. Most of them weren't cold calling, hawking FSBOs, or anything like that. They weren't just lucky–luck might make a good year, but not a good career. And I knew they weren't getting "fed" by their broker, because I was their broker, and I wasn't feeding them!

I can remember when it clicked for me. I was talking with an office manager about the agents in her small office, who had all been doing very well since joining the company. In an off-hand way, she remarked, "I like these agents a lot. They're all really good. I mean, I would list my home with any of them."

That made me stop for a second.

I would list my home with any of them.

As if that was remarkable. As if the idea that a manager would be willing to list her own home with all the agents in her charge was notable in some way.

But it was! It really was! Let's be honest—if you're an experienced agent, you know that you wouldn't list your home with many of the agents who work in your market. Indeed, when I speak to large audiences of agents, I often start by asking how many of them would work with more than half of the agents in their market. I've asked that question to dozens of audiences, thousands of agents. No one raises their hands. No one.

So this manager saying that she would work with any of her agents was actually making a pretty profound observation: these agents were all really good at their jobs.

And it clicked. That's what really successful agents have in common: I would work as a client with any of them. I would trust them with my own personal business. Why? Because they're really great at their jobs. They're professional. They work hard. They know their stuff. When they take a listing, it sells. When they work with a serious buyer, they find her a home. When they get a deal in contract, it closes. And their clients love—absolutely love—them.

That's why they are successful. They are great real estate agents.

Seriously. Go look at the list of the top agents in your office or your market. What you'll find is that most of them are agents that you would trust with your own home sale or a referral of a close friend, precisely because they're great at the job of helping clients buy or sell homes. Yes, maybe you'll find one or two agents who are complete charlatans, who burn every deal they come across, who get by with expensive marketing, or an appetite for endless prospecting, or just the sheer cunning to fool clients into thinking they got a good deal. But they're the exceptions that prove the rule. In general, in my experience, productive agents are great at their jobs.

So how did they get there? How did they become so proficient at helping people buy and sell houses? In many cases, they were doing the things that we're going to talk about in this book.

But I'm not saying that they learned it from me. Rather, I learned it from them! I learned by watching what the most successful agents in my company, and my market, did to build their businesses. And from those experiences, I synthesized a program built on the foundation of being great at your job.

Indeed, when I speak to groups of agents, I invariably hear from some of them, the really successful ones, about how I'm not telling them something they don't already know. They're not trying to insult me, they're simply expressing how they feel validated to finally hear someone encourage them to do what they've always done: do great work and trust that the business will come.

That's what this book is about: helping you become a better real estate agent, a great real estate agent. Because great agents will always get work. They always eventually succeed.

So let's be great.

Introduction

THE CORE
FORMULA

1. THINK EXPANSIVELY ABOUT WHAT PEOPLE NEED.

2. THINK CREATIVELY ABOUT HOW TO SATISFY THE NEED.

3. EXECUTE WELL.

The CORE Formula

"Call me for a Free CMA!"

Ah, yes, the "Free CMA!" For years we saw that offer from real estate agents all over the country, on every business card, every advertisement, every email signature.

So thoughtful!

A market analysis!

For free!

Why did we offer a "Free CMA!" to basically anyone? It'd be nice to think that we were trying to do something useful for people. After all, we know that homeowners are curious about what their home is worth. We pay lip service to the idea that "your home is your most precious investment," so it makes sense that they'd like to keep track of how their home's value changed over time.

In other words, we all recognized that homeowners had a need for our services: the need to know what their home was worth.

And how did we try to address that need?

By giving them the fabulous opportunity to sit through one of our compelling listing presentations!

How nice of us!

Let's be real. We all know that the "Free CMA!" tactic was really just a transparent attempt to lure homeowners into inviting us into their homes, so we could give them a listing presentation in the hopes of persuading them to sell with us. We made the offer because we figured that someone who is willing to call us on it might actually be thinking about putting that home on the market. So sure, we would give them a "Free CMA!" – along with a presentation on our 27-point marketing plan!

And that's why no one ever called on those "Free CMA!" offers. They saw through our clever little ruse. They realized it was the equivalent of those "Free Weekend!" offers you see sometimes at resort hotels, the ones where you get a free room for a few days, but only if you'll sit through a three-hour hard-sell timeshare presentation. They knew that, if they invited you into their home, you were going to try to get them to sell their home. And that's not what they wanted. They just wanted to know what it was worth.

So think about what we did. We recognized that people needed something from us. They wanted to know what their home was worth. But instead of trying to actually satisfy that need, we instead turned it into a prospecting tool to generate a new listing.

And what happened? Zillow happened. The smart people at Zillow recognized that consumers had this need that wasn't being met, and they figured out a way to satisfy that need: the Zestimate! Just go online, put in your address, and get a valuation for your home. Now, we all know that the Zestimate wasn't all that accurate, that arguably it was mostly a click-bait gimmick. But at least Zillow was actually trying to service that client's need, not just using it like we did—as a lure to get some hapless seller tangled in our web.

Indeed, Zillow didn't even have a way to monetize the process, at least not at first. But they figured it out, didn't they? They realized that once they got a lot of eyeballs on their website, and leveraged that with listing data, they could sell ads. And who got monetized? We did! We're the ones paying for it.

You can't blame Zillow for this. It's not their fault that we so foolishly neglected giving our clients something that they needed, leaving them the opening to create a $10 billion (and counting) company at our expense.

No, we have to blame ourselves. We missed it. Why? Because we thought about ourselves, rather than the client.

That's the problem Client-Oriented Real Estate is designed to address. Everything starts with the client. We all need to expand our perspective of what our clients need, rather than what we need. Then we need to think creatively about how we can satisfy those needs: following established best practices or innovating a new way to service them. And then, finally, we need to execute well, following through on the plan and ensuring we give them the kind of service experience that they deserve.

We're going to call this approach the CORE Formula, and break it down into three discrete steps: (1) think expansively about what people need, (2) think creatively about how to create a system to satisfy that need, and (3) execute well. Essentially, this formula is really just a model for a successful business, any kind of business. You look for a void in a market—a consumer need that no one is adequately satisfying. Then you come up with a way to take care of that need, either something new or an improvement on the existing solutions. And then you execute your system to successfully satisfy that need.

That's basically what Zillow did, following that formula to perfection:

1. *Need.* They identified that people needed to know what their home was worth, and even more importantly figured out that no one (like us) was addressing that need.

2. *System.* They found a creative way of satisfying that need by giving consumers one-click instant access to their home value through the Zestimate.

3. *Execution.* They executed well, building an addictive front-end for consumers even while they relentlessly churned through back end data-consistency challenges, constantly improving and expanding the reach of the Zestimate and slowly layering in additional revenue-generating services.

Figure out what people need. Find a system to service the need. Execute well. Seems simple, right? Except that the biggest challenge we face in this industry is that we're not conditioned to think expansively about what our clients need. We're trained to think about our needs: our need for a lead, a listing, a sale.

We need to change that mindset. It's not just Zillow. Consider Angie's List and HomeAdvisor, two companies that saw a gaping need for reliable vendor referrals and ratings. That used to be our job! People used to come to real estate agents when they were looking for landscapers or alarm installers or cleaning services—anything that had to do with the home. But we never put any energy into innovating better ways of servicing that need. And Angie's List and HomeAdvisor stepped into that void. Another opportunity lost.

Just look around. Most of the great businesses we all know became successful by taking an expansive view of what people needed, implementing a creative approach to satisfying those needs, and paying rigorous attention to executing well.

1. Think expansively about what people need.

You start by thinking about what people need. In most cases, you don't even have to be that creative, because lots of needs are obvious and well-established. You just have to find areas where those needs aren't being met.

For example, you might find that your town doesn't have a good dry cleaner, or Indian restaurant, or trusts-and-estates attorneys. So you start up a business to satisfy that marketplace need. You're not "reinventing the wheel," and you're not taking on any extraordinary risks; you're just looking for opportunities to satisfy a well-established but under-served need in a particular market. You can build a pretty good business just looking for those well-known needs that no one is satisfying in your local community.

But the real successes, and the bigger risks, come when you construct a business around a need that's not so well-established or obvious, where you expand your conception of what people are looking for. Whole Foods, for example, saw the opportunity to build a grocery store around the growing consumer need for accessible organic produce. Zipcar realized that people in urban areas didn't just need rental cars once in a while, they needed the ability to "share ownership" of a car. Airbnb saw homeowners needed a way to monetize their homes when they weren't using them. Those needs weren't at all obvious at the time.

Indeed, great businesses sometimes go a step further, and actually create needs that didn't previously exist at all! Take Apple, for example, which became the most successful company in the world by developing products that changed what consumers thought they needed. And they didn't just do it once, they did it three times! We never knew we needed a marketplace to buy digital music files until Apple created the iPod and iTunes. We never knew we needed a miniature computer in our pocket until Apple created the iPhone. And we never knew we needed a handheld tablet computer until Apple created the iPad.

(Unfortunately, of course, we never knew we needed a watch that told us when to stand up and breathe, and we were basically right—Apple can't win them all!)

We never knew we needed any of those gadgets until we had them and then we couldn't live without them. They all seem like foolproof "no-brainers" now, but I can remember the early reviews of the iPad, which many critics derided as simply a larger and more expensive version of an iPod Touch. The critics kind of missed that one. Apple created a market that didn't even exist and manufacturers (including Apple competitors) have now sold over a billion tablets.

Many great companies have similarly created their own consumer need. We never knew we needed frothy variations of cappuccino drinks before Starbucks, and now we routinely carry 20-ounce cups of tasty coffee and cream concoctions around the office. We never knew we absolutely needed products to be shipped overnight until FedEx made it possible, and now we're infuriated if we have to wait any longer. And we never knew that we needed access to warehouse prices (and quantities) until Costco spoiled us, and now we buy cinnamon in 25-pound jars.

Find out what people need now. Even better, think creatively about what they might need in the future. And even better than that, develop a product or system so amazing that it spontaneously generates its own need.

2. Think creatively about how to satisfy that need.

Finding out what people need, though, isn't enough. You also need to create a system or product that satisfies that need. That's how you can build a successful business even if you're addressing a well-established or obvious consumer need: find ways to improve the quality of the product or service that established competitors are using to satisfy that need.

For example, we've already talked about how Angie's List and HomeAdvisor addressed a pretty well-established consumer need for reliable vendor referrals, but created a better system for addressing those needs: an online resource with crowd-sourced reviews and rating systems.

Technological change plays a big role in this, of course, since new technologies create opportunities to address existing needs in innovative ways. Amazon didn't invent the need for retail goods, but created a superior shopping experience: virtually unlimited inventory, product reviews, targeted displays, free two-day-delivery, and all that. Uber built a better taxi service (or, depending on how you look at it, a better limo service) by providing a seamless app interface that allows you to call a car on demand and literally watch as it drives to pick you up. Tesla built a better car, an electric one with a giant tablet as its center console. Better systems, better products.

But it's not just about technology, it's about vision. The wheel, for example, was invented a while ago by some caveman. Nothing new about the wheel. But Bernard D. Sadow, dragging two heavy suitcases through an airport while returning from a Caribbean vacation in 1970, realized how much easier it would be if those cases had wheels. So he created the rolling suitcase, which was a better way of addressing travelers' needs.

And truly great companies find ways to adapt their services as customer needs change around them. HBO, for example, built a business in the 1980s around bringing first-run movies to cable television—most people don't even remember that "HBO" stands for "Home Box Office," playing on the idea that you could watch a movie in your own home. But as more competitors came into that field, HBO had to pivot to stay relevant. People weren't going to pay subscription fees just to watch movies that they could rent from video stores. So HBO started creating its own exclusive content, shows like the Sopranos and Sex and the City, which were only available to subscribers.

3. Execute well.

Finally, you don't even have to be creative in identifying needs or creating systems if you can execute better than anyone else. Most businesses are like that: they don't invent needs or create innovative new systems. Rather, they just follow proven best practices to address a well-known need, and they succeed because they simply execute better.

The incentive for owning a McDonald's franchise, for example, is that you get a proven blueprint for servicing consumers' well-established need for fast food. Indeed, McDonald's won't let you get creative: they don't want you innovating your own way to make a Big Mac, they want you following their established system. But just because you have that proven blueprint doesn't mean your restaurant is guaranteed to succeed. You still have to execute. You have to find the right location, hire the right employees, train them well, and then rigorously follow that McDonald's plan. We've all been to a McDonald's restaurant where the employees were indifferent, or the lines were long, or the bathrooms were filthy.

Execution matters. Nordstrom, for example, is "just" a department store, like a lot of other department stores. It looks the same and has a lot of the same old stuff. But shopping at Nordstrom is qualitatively different because of the way that the company executes on its plan for providing a superior customer experience. Danny Meyer's Union Square restaurant group has thrived in a brutally exacting industry simply by adhering to higher standards of hospitality. You can visit lots of theme parks, but Disney is different. You can stay at a lot of hotels, but not all of them are the Four Seasons.

Companies like Nordstrom, Disney, or the Four Seasons aren't identifying underserved needs. The world is full of department stores, amusement parks, and hotels. And they're not really creating systems that service those needs in innovative, unique ways. Rather, they just do a better job of creating great customer experiences by executing on familiar systems servicing relatively common needs.

Case Study: The Video Rental Business

George Atkinson changed your life. You probably don't even know who he is, but he created an industry that's become an essential part of the way we live today.

In our on-demand culture, we can all watch any movie or television show ever made with a few taps on our phones, tablets, or remotes. But it wasn't always that way. Back in the dark ages, when I was growing up, movies came out in the theaters, and then they just disappeared. For years and years! At some point, they might turn up on broadcast television as a "Movie of the Week," or maybe they'd get re-released for a short theatrical run, but, otherwise, you simply never saw them again.

Imagine that! What a primitive way to live! It's almost unimaginable to kids today that we couldn't just pull up just about any movie ever released anytime we wanted.

That all started to change in the 1970s, with the invention of the video-cassette recorder. People suddenly had devices in their homes that could not only record live television, but also play pre-recorded tapes of old Hollywood films. This was a ground-breaking invention, but it didn't by itself solve the movie-on-demand problem for most consumers. Why? Because studios were slow to license their movies for sale to the general public, fearing that they would cannibalize the lucrative theater markets. And even when studios started licensing their movies to distributors, they priced the tapes at exorbitantly expensive levels, often hundreds of dollars each, making them difficult purchases for most families.

That's when Atkinson had his life-changing idea. He had a background in the niche business leasing the traditional reel-to-reel versions of theatrical releases for special events, and he realized that he could adapt that same model for the general public: buy the movies, then rent them out to a customer for the night. So he bought a bunch of tapes, took out an ad advertising his "video rental club," and started renting movies out. Eventually, he built a company called "Video Station" that essentially created the video rental industry. He made a lot of money, and deserved to.

After Atkinson paved the way, "mom-and-pop" video rental shops followed, flourishing in neighborhoods all over the country.

Most followed his established business model: buy a bunch of tapes, start a club, rent them out. This was the beginning of widespread video-on-demand, because almost everyone had easy access to at least one independent video shop that could rent them hundreds, if not thousands, of movies.

But these mom-and-pop shops had their limitations. They were usually small stores, with a limited selection of movies and a small number of copies for each. So they would routinely run out of high-demand titles like new releases.

And then came Blockbuster. You might not even remember Blockbuster, which exploded across the country in the mid-1980s with a new-and-improved business model that addressed the inherent weakness in the independent video store system: lots and lots and lots of movies in big, beautiful, well-lit stores. An old classic? They had it. The latest new release? They had it. They had everything. Blockbuster basically used economies of scale to create a better system for satisfying the need for on-demand video, and built an empire that, at its peak, had over 9,000 stores and was worth over $8 billion. "Let's make it a Blockbuster Night" became the slogan of an era for couch potatoes all over the country.

But Blockbuster had a flaw in its business model as well, particularly in its revenue model. Specifically, Blockbuster over-relied on gimmicky charges to make a profit. You could rent a movie cheaply, but your costs could easily skyrocket. Let's say, for example, that you forgot to rewind the tape when you were done. That's an extra few bucks. And heaven forbid you forget to return the movie by the due date. Those late fees could really add up.

That's actually how Blockbuster made their profit: junk charges like rewinding penalties and late fees. They were like credit card companies, which make their money not from people who pay their bill off every month, but from the ones who roll their balances over month after month and build up escalating finance charges. Customers became addicted to Blockbuster, but they resented those junk charges.

Unfortunately for Blockbuster, one of those unhappy consumers was an entrepreneur named Reed Hastings. Legend has it that in 1997, Reed kept his rental of *Apollo 13* for about six weeks too long and was forced to pay a $40 late fee. Unhappy with the experience and looking for an opportunity to start up a new business, Hastings founded a competing video rental company. He called it "Netflix."

You've definitely heard of Netflix, right? You probably think of it as a streaming service, which is what it does today. But back in the 1990s, Netflix devastated Blockbuster with a much more prosaic business model: rent DVDs with no junk fees. Netflix was originally an online subscription service that allowed you to order several DVDs at a time and then keep them for as long as you wanted. When you watched one, you'd mail it back to Netflix in a special envelope they gave you, and they'd send you the next movie in your online queue. An unlimited selection, no schlepping to the store, and no return deadlines. Simply put, Netflix out-innovated Blockbuster in the same way that Blockbuster eclipsed the mom-and-pop shops.

Today, of course, that DVD subscription service that was so revolutionary at the time, and which eventually helped drive Blockbuster into bankruptcy, is a small part of Netflix's revenue. In fact, many people don't even realize that Netflix was originally a DVD subscription service. Heck, many people don't even know what a DVD is!

Why? Because consumer needs eventually changed, as streaming technology became a viable way of delivering movies on demand. That evolution could have doomed Netflix, but they were smart and nimble enough to adapt to the changing technology and create the dominant platform for on-demand video. And then they evolved again, developing their own exclusive content to bring even more value to their users. Today, they have over 100 million subscribers and earn over $8 billion in revenue each year.

The CORE Formula and Real Estate

The history of the video rental industry over the past 40 years illustrates the "need, system, execute" foundation of the CORE Formula, and what we need to do to implement a client-oriented philosophy in the real estate industry:

First, we have to think expansively about what people need. George Atkinson created an industry that did not previously exist because he realized that people needed an affordable way to watch movies-on-demand in the comfort of their homes. No one else saw that need. He did.

Moreover, we have to be able to adapt as those needs change over time. People needed to watch movies at home. Then they needed to have access to all the first-run new releases the week they became available. Then they didn't want to pay late fees or schlep to the store. Then they didn't even want to have to put DVDs in an envelope. Consumer needs change, particularly as technology changes, and you have to be able to adapt.

Similarly, in the real estate industry, we have to think expansively about what our clients need, especially in situations where no one is satisfying those needs. We can't miss any more opportunities the way that we ceded the "how much is my home worth?" question to Zillow. We need to be careful to adapt as needs change, particularly if new technology makes better service systems possible. And, of course, we should be on the lookout for opportunities to create needs that may not even exist yet, in the same way that Atkinson created his own consumer demand for movie rentals, Apple the need for tablets, and Starbucks the need for frothy coffees.

Second, we have to think creatively about how to service those needs. Atkinson created a system that made video rentals affordable. Blockbuster created a better system, one that used economies of scale to ensure that consumers could rent just about any movie they wanted. And Netflix created an even better system, with essentially unlimited inventory and the elimination of late fees and trips to the store. Ultimately, of course, Netflix created an even better system when it became an early provider of streaming video.

We have to be just as creative in developing systems to satisfy real estate consumer needs. We have to stop putting all our innovative energy and money into lead generation and start focusing on how we can provide better products and services for our clients. Netflix improved the video rental system. Uber improved car service. Amazon improved the retail experience. How can we improve the real estate transaction?

Third, we have to execute those systems well. Today, we remember Blockbuster as a business school case study for its failure to adapt to changing needs and technologies, but we shouldn't forget just how dominant and popular it was in its time. Blockbuster knew how to execute: convenient locations, clever marketing, beautiful stores, and a brilliant-if-doomed method of wringing revenue out of hapless subscribers. The first Blockbuster store opened in 1985. Nine years later, Viacom bought the chain for $8.4 billion. That's a pretty good run for a company whose main innovation was applying economies of scale to an established "mom-and-pop" business model. Yes, it ultimately went under when it failed to adapt its business model to changing needs and technology. But, in its heyday, Blockbuster was a massive success story because of its rigorous execution.

Similarly, we have to find ways to ensure better execution of best practices for ensuring a superior client service experience. We have to overcome the challenges of enforcing system compliance in an industry dominated by independent contractors and find a way to provide more consistently great experiences. We don't have a "Four Seasons of real estate," and we need one.

Conclusion

How do we get there? How do we become the gold standard for client service in the real estate industry? We follow the CORE Formula: (1) think expansively about what people need, (2) build creative systems that can service those needs, and (3) develop rigorous methods to ensure that we execute well.

That's what we're going to do in this book. We're going to take the CORE Formula and apply it to the three major inflection points in the real estate business: how we generate leads, how we convert those leads into clients, and then how we service those clients through the transactional process.

But because we're now expanding our conceptions about what people need and how we can give it to them, we're going to re-frame those inflection points from a more client-oriented perspective:

Part One: Client Development. How we can grow our business by expanding our conception of who our clients are, and by focusing on the services we can provide to them, as a way of cultivating the kinds of relationships that generate business opportunities.

Part Two: Client Conversion. How we can take a consultative approach to the classic listing and buyer presentations by orienting them around the client, not ourselves, specifically by talking less and listening more, articulating a more modern value proposition, and taking a collaborative approach to pricing.

Part Three: Client Management. How we manage the client experiences of our buyers and sellers by expanding our conception of what they need, creating best practice protocols to service those needs, and then executing on those protocols through well-designed Action Plans.

Be great at developing clients. Be great at consulting with your clients. Be great at taking care of your clients.

Just be great at your job.

So let's get started.

Part One:
Client Development

Chapter 1

Who's Your Agent?

L̲e̲t̲'s̲ s̲t̲a̲r̲t̲ w̲i̲t̲h̲ s̲o̲m̲e̲ s̲i̲m̲p̲l̲e̲ q̲u̲e̲s̲t̲i̲o̲n̲s̲.

Who's your accountant?

If I met you at a cocktail party and told you I needed an accountant to help me pay my taxes, do you have a name that you'd give me? Okay, great! Because the government appreciates your financial support.

Who's your dentist?

You do have a dentist, right? I mean, I hope you do. If you don't, you should probably just put the book down right now and go find yourself a dentist, because that's just not healthy. Seriously. Go right now. We'll wait. Your health comes first.

Who's your hair stylist?

I've asked that question to a lot of audiences, and I generally find that most men can't give me a name, because many of them are bald and most of the rest are filthy animals that don't care how they look. But women—they almost always have a hair stylist, usually someone they've gone to for a long time. So they have a name.

Okay, here's where we stand: you've told me that you have an accountant, and a dentist, and maybe a hair stylist.

Now, just one more question:

How many people would say that you're their real estate agent?

Think about it. If I came to your town and started haranguing people on the street with these questions, how many of those people would have a name for their accountant, dentist, and hair stylist? Probably most of them, right? And many of them could probably also name their doctor, plumber, electrician, architect, and all sorts of other service professionals.

But how many of them would also name you as their real estate agent?

Honestly, how many of them would name *anyone* as their real estate agent?

I'll tell you what would happen, because I've actually done this.

Most people have an accountant.

Almost all of them have a dentist.

All the women have a hair stylist.

And almost nobody has a real estate agent.

Even if they do have a real estate agent, it's because they're actually in the process of selling or buying a home right at that moment: they're listed or looking.

But if they bought a few years ago? Then they don't think of themselves as "having" a real estate agent. They "had" a real estate agent, but not anymore. Their transaction is over, and that relationship has ended.

Why is that? Why do people think of themselves as "having" an accountant, dentist, a hair stylist, or other service professional, but don't think they "have" a real estate agent?

You might think it's just about the frequency of a transaction. After all, most people (hopefully!) do their taxes every year and (hopefully!) see their dentist twice a year. And they go to the hair stylist every few months or so, or at least whenever their roots start to show. But most people take years and years between real estate transactions, so that naturally frays whatever connection they might have to their agent.

Okay, maybe that's part of it. But people "have" a lot of service professionals that they only see infrequently. You don't generally need a plumber or an electrician every year, or an architect, or a plastic surgeon. But once you've established a relationship with a professional you like and trust, you tend to think of them as "your" provider, even if you don't need your pipes cleared or your face lifted every year. The relationship exists outside the transaction.

In real estate, though, the relationship usually ends when the transaction closes. Part of it is that most agents don't work very hard to keep that relationship going. They generally focus their energies and attention on "leads," endlessly prospecting for people who might be buying or selling within the next six months.

It's understandable, of course: we focus on transactions because that's when we get paid. I get it. But that relentless drive to generate leads sometimes makes us obsess too much about the short-term. A neighbor stops by our open house because she is curious about the layout and we dismiss her as a "looky-loo." We don't follow up with that call on our listing once we realize they're not looking to move anytime soon. And even though we love those wonderful clients who just bought a house from us, well, they're not going to be moving again anytime soon, are they? So why spend a lot of time on them?

Even worse, because we think transactionally, consumers think transactionally. If we don't pay attention to them, they're not going to pay attention to us. Indeed, rather than see us as service professionals like lawyers or plumbers, they see us strictly as "salespeople"—the "Original Sin." There's nothing inherently wrong with that; after all, sales are a part of what we do. But the problem is that no one "has" a salesperson. People don't feel loyalty to a salesperson.

Think of it this way: if you were in the market to buy a car, would you be committed to working with the salesperson who sold you your last car? Not really. No one runs around saying, "you have to buy a car from my guy at Audi!" or "if you're buying clothes, you have to go see Nancy at Macy's—she's the very best!" We simply don't maintain relationships with salespeople the same way we do with service professionals like accountants, dentists, hair stylists, and the rest.

That's why both agents and consumers share a narrow conception of what real estate agents do for clients: help you transact real estate. We think transactionally because that's when we get paid. And people think transactionally because they don't generally maintain ongoing relationships with salespeople.

And by extension, both agents and consumers share a narrow conception of what clients need from agents: assistance in transacting real estate. Essentially, people don't "have" a real estate agent because they think that they only need an agent if they're actively in the market. If they're not buying or selling real estate right now, they don't *need* an agent.

Here's the problem with that way of thinking: it's just not true. People have real estate needs that go well beyond just a real estate transaction. They're not necessarily needs that will generate a sales commission, but they're still real estate needs.

Here, I can prove it to you.

The "Cocktail Party Conversation"

Let's say that you're at a cocktail party, or a kid's soccer game, or at a networking event, or hanging out after church or temple or mosque or Satanic Temple, or whatever. The important thing is that you're in a social situation where you meet someone you don't already know. If you can think back to the last time you had a conversation like that, here's what probably happened.

Because you're a sociable person, you probably asked them about themselves and their work. So you asked:

So what do you do?

And they said something like:

I'm a florist.

Or an accountant, or a bartender, or whatever. The point is that they're going to tell you what they do. So now, you ask them a few more questions about their work, where they live, things like that. If you're a good conversationalist, of course, you know that the best way to build rapport with people is to ask them questions about themselves. So that's what you did. Then, at some point in the conversation, that florist turned the question back on you. He asked:

And what do you do?

And you said:

I'm in real estate.

Okay, stop!

Seriously, I want you to think about the last time you had a conversation like that, where you told someone you didn't know that you were in real estate. What's the next question out of their mouths?

Do you remember it?

It was almost certainly this one:

How's the market?

You get asked that all the time, don't you? If you introduce yourself to someone, and tell them you're in real estate, they ask you how the market is. Not once in a while. Not sometimes. Not most times. Almost all the time.

Indeed, because I'm both a lawyer and a real estate broker, I have a couple of different ways that I can answer the "what do you do?" question. I've found that if I don't really want to talk to that person,

I just tell them I'm a lawyer. That usually ends things. No one wants to talk to a lawyer.

But if I want to get into a conversation, I tell them I'm a real estate broker. Because I know the next thing out of their mouth will be:

How's the market?

That's a really important question, because it tells us a few things about consumers. For one thing, they're curious about what's going on in the real estate market. They want to know if it's up or down, hot or cold, busy or slow. And that makes sense, because everyone is in the real estate market. They all live somewhere. If they live with their parents, they want to know what's happening with rentals. If they rent, they probably have hopes of someday buying. If they own, they want to know how their investment is doing, and maybe, just maybe, they're thinking of upsizing or downsizing.

The real estate market is unique in that way: not everyone owns stocks, not everyone owns bonds, but everyone has to live somewhere. That's why they're always asking real estate agents, "How's the market?"

That's what we call the "Cocktail Party Conversation" question: you meet someone new, tell someone what you do, and they ask, "How's the market?" It's a really important conversation, because it tells us that people have at least one specific need that goes well beyond the real estate transaction—the need to know how the market is doing.

But the "Cocktail Party Conversation" tells us something even more important: this need isn't being met. These people want to know what's going on in the market, and no one is telling them.

Why? Because they don't "have" an agent. They don't have someone they can turn to when they have real estate questions, someone they can rely on, someone they can trust.

And they need one! They need an agent. If they had an agent, they wouldn't be asking random agents like you how the market is doing, would they? They'd already know.

It's not just about keeping track of the real estate market. Think of all the non-transactional real estate questions that consumers have every day. They pass a "for sale" sign on their block, they want to know what the house is selling for. They see it come down, they want to know the sold price. They have questions about their taxes and their mortgage. They need recommendations for a plumber or an electrician or some other professional. They want to know how much their home is worth, maybe for a tax grievance or an insurance valuation. And, at any given time, they're thinking of adding another bedroom, or finishing their basement, or putting in a pool, or doing any number of home improvement projects that might impact their property value. Shouldn't they talk to a real estate agent before they spend $50,000 on a new kitchen, just to get an idea of whether they're making a good long-term investment?

And yet, these people rarely call an agent for help. Why? Oddly enough, it's usually because they're too nice. They don't want to bother the agent with questions that don't involve buying or selling. They realize that we only get paid on a transaction, and they're reluctant to "take advantage" of us by asking for free advice. They think of agents as salespeople who help them through a transaction, not as resources for information on all things real estate.

We can't blame them because that's how we think of ourselves. Consumers are simply following our lead. We think transactionally, so they think transactionally. We pay attention to them only when they're buying or selling, so they pay attention to us only when they're buying or selling.

But isn't it a little convenient that we've chosen to define consumer real estate needs as limited to the need to buy or sell a home? Yes, that's the only time they're willing to pay us, but it's not the only time they need us.

Remember that being great at your job starts with a simple guideline: think expansively about what people need. Well, the Cocktail Party conversation shows you that everyone needs a real estate agent. A great real estate agent. All the time. Even when they're not buying or selling.

And that great real estate agent should be you.

Who Would You Call?

So apply for that job. They need a real estate agent. And, as it happens, you're a real estate agent.

The florist says:

How's the market?

You say:

Well, it all depends on your individual situation. Do you own or rent right now?

That's really the only answer to the question. It depends on the situation. As real estate professionals, we always want a hot market, with sales and prices going up, so we sometimes say that the market is "doing great!" when it's busy. Why? Because it's great for us! Very agent-oriented.

But a busy market is not so great for people who aren't home-owners yet. They'd obviously rather see a slower market with prices flat or falling.

So if you don't know someone's personal situation, you have to find out. As always, CORE teaches us to focus on other people's needs, not our own. Thus, your answer to "How's the market?" is always "It depends."

That usually gets that florist to open up. Maybe he owns something. Maybe he's renting. Maybe he's living in his mom's basement. Whatever. Everyone lives somewhere, which means that everyone's in the real estate market.

Depending on what he says, you give him your read on the market: is it hot or cold, are sales going up or down, what's happening with pricing, that sort of thing? In other words, answer the question.

And once you've answered his question, you get to yours, which is a really important one:

Hey, can I ask you, who's your real estate agent?

"Who's your real estate agent?" Great question. Remember, he has an accountant, a dentist, maybe a hair stylist. But does he have a real estate agent? Probably not. As we've established, very few people think of themselves as having a real estate agent if they're not actively in the market to buy or sell something. Even better, it's the kind of question that can't be answered with a simple "yes" or "no."

Here's what he's probably going to say:

Oh, no, I don't have an agent. But I'm not looking to sell right now.

Now, he's a little nervous, because he thinks you're going to give him some aggressive sales-y solicitation, that you're going to try to get him to sell his house right then and there. He literally might back away from you a little, his body language telling you that he's now on high alert, Sales-Con-1.

But that's not where you're going with this. Instead of a sales solicitation, you use what we'll think of as the "Who Would You Call...?" Dialogue.

No, of course you're not selling. I figured that. It's funny that people think they only need a real estate agent when they're buying or selling. But I think that people need an agent all the time.

Let me ask you, who would you call if you were thinking of putting in a new kitchen and wanted to know how it would affect your property value? Or who would you call if you were adding a pool, or finishing your basement, and wanted to know how it might affect your resale value?

"Who would you call...?"

Another great question! It can't be answered with a "yes" or a "no," and 90% of the time they're not going to be able to give you a name. Instead, they say something like this:

Well, no, I don't have anyone I'd call.

Of course they don't. No one does. Almost no one "has" a real estate agent.

So you can say:

Okay, well, now you do! I'd be happy to be your resource when you have questions like that. I have a whole "friends and family" group of people like you who aren't buying or selling but want to stay on top of what's happening with the market and the community. I'll be happy to add you. I promise I won't spam you or anything like that.

It's really that simple. The dialogue I've provided is just an example of how that conversation might go. Find your own words, your own cadence. The key points are simple:

- You ask, "Who's your real estate agent?"

- They (probably) say, "I don't have one."

- And you say, "well, who would you call...?" with whatever hook you think will resonate:

Who would you call... if you were thinking of putting in a new kitchen

Who would you call... if you were thinking of adding a bedroom?

Who would you call... if you were thinking of building a pool?

Who would you call... if you wanted to grieve your taxes?

Who would you call... if you saw a house for sale in your neighborhood and wanted to know what it was selling for?

Who would you call... if you needed a valuation for your insurance?

Who would you call... if you needed a recommendation for a handyman/electrician/plumber/landscaper/etc.?

In other words, make it clear to them that they don't have an agent to call about those questions and that they probably need one. And if you then ask them for their contact information within that context, they're much more likely to give it to you, because you're offering to bring something of value to them.

You just need to be careful not to come on too strong and to reassure them that you're not trying to sell them something. For example, the one question you should never ask is this: "Who would you call if you were thinking of moving?" Sure, it would be nice to know that, but that's the solicitation that the florist was afraid of. That's not information that's helpful to him, it's information helpful only to you. Don't worry. You're not missing anything. They're not moving. If they were moving, they would have mentioned that already.

When do you use the "Who Would You Call?" dialogue? You should use it every day. Every single day. Every time you meet someone you don't know that you think needs a real estate agent. When you meet florists at cocktail parties. When you come across looky-loos at open houses. When you realize that the person who clicked on "find out more" on one of your listings isn't really interested in moving anytime soon.

You meet them. You get their information. You get their consent.

What's the worst that happens? They say no. No harm done. You tried.

But if they say "yes"? Now, you're getting somewhere. Because now you've got someone you can add to what we call your "Sphere of Support."

Chapter 2

The Sphere of Support: They're All Clients

MY LATE FATHER WAS A DOCTOR FOR ABOUT 30 YEARS and developed an immensely successful medical practice. His patients absolutely loved him, and he loved them back.

About five years after he retired, we were walking through a local mall. Suddenly, a woman came up to us, greeting him enthusiastically, giving him a hug. They talked for a bit, just social chit-chat. Later, when she left, I asked him who she was.

He said, "she's a patient."

Now, my father at that point had been retired for years, and probably hadn't even seen that particular patient for a few years before that. But it didn't matter. She was still his patient. She would always be his patient. Not literally – if she'd asked him to write a prescription for her, he would have politely declined. She wasn't under his care at the time. But his mindset was clear: she was a "patient." And in that same way, her mindset was clear: he was her doctor.

That's how we need to think about the people in our lives. They're clients even if they're not buying or selling right now. And we should treat them that way: attending to their needs even when they're not in the market for the simple reason that they're your clients, and you should take care of them. That's our job.

Listen, I know what you're thinking: "That's my job? That doesn't sound like such a good job! Why do I want to be a real estate agent for people who aren't even buying or selling? You want me to do all this work for free?"

Yes, that's precisely what I want you to do. Work for free. Why? Because no one ever paid for the Zestimate either. And yet, by addressing consumers' need to know what their home was worth, Zillow built a relationship with those consumers. They visited the site once, then visited again, then bookmarked it, then got the app, and eventually started to think of Zillow as their "go to" resource for real estate information. The relationships that Zillow forged with its user base had value and, eventually, Zillow figured out a way to monetize that value.

So should we. We all have durable, existing relationships with our friends, family, past clients, current clients, neighbors, former work colleagues, and other people in our communities. Those relationships have value.

We also have less tangible but potential relationships with all the random people we come into contact with in our work: the looky-loo open house visitors from Sunday, the unrepresented FSBO seller we called last month, the long list of people who we usually think of as "dead leads" because they weren't really in the market at the time we talked to them. And, yes, that florist from the Cocktail Party Conversation. Those relationships have value, too.

And the key to realizing that value is simple: treat them all like my dad treated his patients. Treat them like clients.

Adopt them as your clients, position yourself as their real estate agent, and follow the CORE Formula: think expansively about what they need, creatively about how you can give it to them, and then execute as if they're paying you—even if they're not. Foster a dynamic in which they start to believe they "have" a real estate agent just like they have an accountant and a dentist and a hair stylist.

Now, I don't mean that you should *literally* treat everyone like a client. You're not going to meet someone at a Cocktail Party and then give them a bunch of disclosures to sign. You're not going to assume a fiduciary responsibility for a seller that hasn't signed a listing with you yet, any more than my father would have given that patient a prescription. I'm just talking about your attitude, your mindset, your approach.

That's how you build a great business. Create relationships, cultivate relationships, and develop relationships. They have value. Maybe you won't realize that value today, or tomorrow, but eventually you'll get something from the work you put in.

Why? Because everyone moves eventually. All those people that you cultivate as your "non-transactional clients," will eventually become "transactional clients"—or, at least, you'll have the opportunity to convert them into transactional clients. And positioning yourself as someone's real estate agent is the best way to earn their business: if you can forge a relationship with them by simply being a resource to answer their real estate questions, or to provide them with unpaid non-transactional services, they're more likely to turn to you when they need paying, transactional services.

Think of it this way: are you planning on being in the business in five years? Ten years? If so, wouldn't it be nice to depend on a handful (or more) deals every year from these non-transactional clients that you've invested small amounts of money and time in every year? Isn't it worth doing a little work this year, and next year, and the year after that, for a piece of business you can close in five years?

Ultimately, it's always going to be more cost- and time-effective to cultivate those existing relationships than to try to start new ones. It's a standard business cliché: it costs a lot more to acquire a new client than it does to retain an existing one. Just think about all the money and energy you probably spend trying to generate leads. Wouldn't it be a lot easier and cheaper to cultivate deeper relationships with your existing clients—or, at least, the people that should be your clients—if you actually opened up your perspective to treat everyone in your life, and everyone you meet through your business, as a client?

The point is, you already have a lot of clients, and you meet new ones every day. You just don't treat them like clients, so they don't think of you as their real estate agent.

At least, not yet.

But they will.

The Sphere of ~~Influence~~ Support

I never liked the term "Sphere of Influence." That's the way traditional sales gurus describe that "friends and family" group of people that you cultivate for direct business and referrals. In old-fashioned prospecting, you "work" your "Sphere of Influence" by exerting that purported influence, calling and mailing them periodically to find out when they're moving, or if they know anyone who is buying or selling right now.

But the term "Sphere of Influence" has always seemed kind of sinister to me, like you're some sort of Svengali who is going to mesmerize people into doing business with you, waving your arms at them going "Wooohooooo, you're getting very sleepy, now you're under my influence..."

Indeed, the whole idea of a "Sphere of Influence" was an agent-oriented way of thinking about the relationship between you and your clients, like you were their center of gravity and they were orbiting around your star. It was about treating them as an instrument of your influence, not respecting their own agency, their own personhood. It was about you, not them.

So we're going to take a much more client-oriented approach to the Sphere, changing it from a "Sphere of Influence" to a "Sphere of Support." Because it's not about exerting influence over people, it's about supporting them. Essentially, we want you to create a reciprocal relationship with the people you know: you support them with services when they're not buying or selling and, hopefully, they support you when they are. You treat them like clients and hope that they'll think of you as their agent.

You give support, and then you get support. That's the Sphere of Support.

Who goes into the Sphere? Well, just about everyone. The Sphere is essentially a clearinghouse for contacts, the place where you store information on every possible person who might do a piece of business with you during the long course of your career.

Think of it this way: Everyone you know and everyone you meet can be sorted into one of three categories:

- *Active Clients.* These are the contacts who are thinking of buying or selling in the near-future. You don't put them in the Sphere of Support, because you're going to want to cultivate them much more aggressively for appointments to turn them into active buyers or listings. They belong in a lead follow-up program, not the Sphere.

- *Non-Clients.* These are the contacts whose information you retain, but whom you're not going to consider clients: people who ask to be removed from your marketing lists, who tell you they have an agent, other real estate agents, and anyone else who isn't going to be part of a service-and-marketing program. Essentially, these are the people in your "Address Book" who aren't going to be part of your Sphere of Support. You need their information (i.e., the phone number of an agent you did a deal with), but you're not going to be servicing their needs or marketing to them.

- *The Sphere of Support.* This is pretty much everyone else: (1) anyone you know, (2) who knows you, (3) from your market area, (4) for whom you have good contact information, and (5) who gives you permission to market to them.

Let's break those five Sphere criteria down:

1. *Anyone you know.* You actually have to know who they are. Don't go dumping some random list of local residents or some call sheet for your kid's school into your Sphere.

2. *Who knows you.* You don't need to be friends, or even acquaintances. Heck, you might never have met in person. But they should know who you are and recognize your name.

3. *Who is in your market area.* The whole Sphere marketing campaign is geared toward your local market, so you're not going to be able to do much for anyone outside of it. (If you work a vacation/resort market, though, you might expand this concept to include anyone *interested* in your market area.)

4. *For whom you have good contact information.* As you'll see, the marketing and service program for your Sphere requires email and mobile phone contact information. If you don't have it and can't get it, they don't belong in the Sphere.

5. *Who gives you permission to market to them.* You don't need formal permission or a signed disclosure, just an okay from them that they're willing to accept you as a resource for real estate information. You can get the permission when you meet them or you can go to the people you already know and ask them if it's okay.

Essentially, your Sphere of Support is a database consisting of everyone you're going to consider a client—which is almost everyone with whom you have even a glancing personal relationship. So that includes not only everyone you know right now, but anyone you meet going forward: the dentist at the party, the looky-loo who came your open house, the online lead who ducks your calls for weeks before finally picking up, the sign caller who says she's not ready for a few years—everyone. If you have contact information for them and they give you permission to add them to the list, they go in the Sphere.

So that's the "Sphere." Now, let's talk about the "Support."

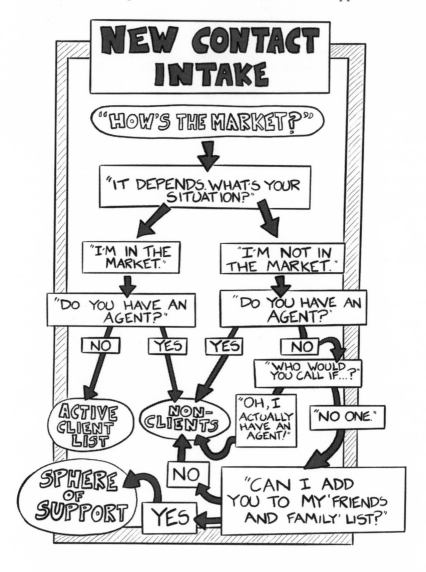

Giving Support: the CORE Courtesy Services

We call it the "Sphere of Support" because you're going to be providing support to your non-transactional clients—the ones who aren't actually buying or selling right now.

That's the whole idea of Client-Oriented Real Estate: expand our conception of what people need and think creatively about the services we can provide to service those needs. We've already expanded our conception of what these non-transactional clients need: they need a real estate agent! So now, let's think creatively about the services we can provide to satisfy those needs:

1. *Real Estate Market Information.* Whether they're homeowners, sellers, buyers, or just observers, everyone is interested in the real estate market. And, as their agent, you should provide them with regular updates to satisfy that need: market trends, home valuation, neighborhood news, and the like. Give them access to an online valuation with alerts anytime that value changes. Let them know what that home down the block sold for. Send out advisories about tax changes, interest rate updates, things like that.

2. *Property Management.* Most people need advice about property management. Certainly, no one should ever do any kind of home improvement without at least considering the impact on their property values, and a local real estate agent is the best person to provide that consultation. Even non-homeowners, though, still need to maintain the home they live in. So they need an agent to advise them about their schedule of routine maintenance, and to be a resource for professional referrals for everything relating to the home: landscapers, alarm system providers, plumbers, electricians, general contractors, etc.

3. *Community Information.* As real estate brokers and agents, we literally "live off the land." That is, we make our living based on the desirability of the local communities we serve. If more people want to live where we work, then demand goes up, transactions increase, property values rise, and we become more successful. That's why real estate

professionals have traditionally thought of themselves as stewards of their local communities and have taken leadership in promoting those communities. So take ownership of your local area, advising people about local events, programs, services, and things like that.

Collectively, we call these three services the "CORE Courtesy Services," because we provide them free of charge as a courtesy to the people in our Sphere of Support. If you're going to be a client's real estate agent, even when they're not buying or selling, then you need to take ownership of what's happening in real estate, with their own property, and in the community they live in.

Why call them the "Courtesy" Services? Think about what a courtesy is: a sign of respect, of politeness, of consideration, of manners. It's doing something good for someone for no reason other than it's the right thing to do, often tangentially related to what we do for a living. A real estate lawyer gets paid to work on legal documents, but will often notarize a document as a courtesy. Hotels charge for hospitality, but will direct you to their lobby bathroom even if you're not staying there. Electronics stores sell computers but will usually answer your questions about why your laptop is on the fritz even if you're not planning on buying anything.

Why do they do that? Why do they work for free? Because they incur a minimal cost in providing that service, and they'd rather generate the goodwill as a means of building a relationship with a potential customer or client. Plus, it's a nice thing to do, and most people are nice.

And that's you! You're nice! So even though you're not getting paid for it, you can provide these Courtesy Services to the people you know as a means of generating goodwill and developing that relationship. That's not only your mindset, but it's also the framing you want to cultivate in your clients—that you're providing these services as a courtesy to them because you value them. That's the way to build that relationship, to position yourself as their agent.

The Service-and-Marketing Program

Here's the most important thing you need to remember about marketing to the people in your Sphere:

Don't be annoying.

Too much real estate marketing is really annoying. Why? Because it's agent-oriented, not client-oriented. Agents send marketing that is interesting and important to them, not to the people they're inflicting it on. And because digital marketing through email and social media is basically free and easy, their annoyingness is essentially unrestrained by the limitations of time or money.

For example, agents routinely blast out their new listing to their entire mailing list, or throw it out on social media to their entire friends list, even though most of those people aren't in the market to buy a home and may have little interest in either the price point or market area of the listing. Now, if you're sending out that listing to a targeted list of buyers based on price range and location, that's a terrific service to both your seller and those interested purchasers. But the people on your Sphere are by definition not thinking of buying or selling a home in the near future. If they were actually in the market, you'd be working with them as an active client, doing a lot more than sending them passive marketing. So why are you sending them a new listing? To prove that you actually take listings, that you're a successful real estate agent? It's like doing a touchdown dance: maybe it's better to act like you've been there before.

Now, I get it that personal branding is important and you want to promote your listing, but nothing is more irritating than surfing through a social media feed or inbox littered with blatant solicitations for business. It's almost like a breach of a social contract: if you want to advertise, pay for the privilege. I didn't friend you on Facebook or share my personal email with you so that you could harangue me with your new listings.

So don't be annoying. Don't send out marketing that's only interesting to you—send out marketing that's interesting to them. If you really want to post your new listing, find an angle that makes it more interesting to people who aren't in the market: show off the kitchen, or the view, or some feature about the home as a conversation-starter. Engage people, don't just yap at them.

Even more importantly, send out information that reinforces your role as their real estate agent. Too often, traditional Sphere marketing takes an agent outside her core expertise, like monthly mailings that focus on "how to set a budget," "tips for avoiding procrastination," "great holiday recipes," or things like that. And why do I get 25 email reminders from agents every time I have to change the clocks for Daylight Saving? Those are harmless, I guess, but what do they have to do with real estate? You're not a life coach or a financial planner or a chef or the keeper-of-the-clocks. You're a real estate agent. Stick to your area of expertise. Like, I would love getting mailings from my doctor with medical information, but it wouldn't make much sense to me if she sent me gardening advice.

So in marketing to your Sphere, stick to the three CORE Courtesy Services that reflect your expertise: (1) explaining what's going on in the market, (2) advising on how to manage a home, and (3) promoting the local community. Indeed, let's not even talk about it as a marketing program, but a "Service-and-Marketing" program that provides valuable services to your clients even while promoting you and your business.

The easiest and most common way to implement this kind of program is to create some sort of digital newsletter that you can email out and post on social media every month. You don't even need anything particularly elaborate or fancy, just a basic template that you can fill with information that relates to your core expertise: real estate or community news, market reports, neighborhood activity, online valuations, event announcements, discount offers, vendor/partner lists, and links to your social media and website pages.

The key to providing these services through an effective digital mailing campaign is to be consistent. You need to send something out regularly, not so frequently that you become a pest but often enough that you establish a top-of-mind familiarity. No more than once per week, no less than once per month. You also want to make your system as automatic as possible, part of a routine, so that you don't have to re-think the process every time.

You can find any number of resources that can become the backbone of your digital campaign just by browsing the aisles at your next trade show or convention or looking through the pages of *REALTOR Magazine*. The providers and systems change pretty frequently, so we're not going to recommend a particular service here, but if you go to www.joerand.com we have a resources page that provides a regularly updated guide to some of the programs we recommend.

Ultimately, though, the key to a successful Sphere development campaign is simple: provide a service. Make it about them, not you.

Getting Support

So if that's how you support your Sphere clients, how do they support you? Well, that's pretty obvious—they support you by hiring you when they're ready to buy or sell a home.

The main purpose of the Sphere of Support campaign is to generate direct business. You build an agent-client relationship with people who aren't buying or selling, to generate top-of-mind awareness so that when they do decide to buy or sell, they come to you. If you treat them like they're your clients, they'll start thinking of you as their agent. And if they get used to you providing them non-transactional Courtesy Services, they'll naturally turn to you when they need transactional services.

Think of it this way: the real estate lead generation infrastructure relies on the recognition that most consumers don't have an agent, and will only start looking for one when they are already searching for a home. That's why we put up signs, and build websites, and send mailings, and advertise on portals, and hold open houses, and do all the other stuff we do to generate leads. We want to try to grab their attention when they do start thinking about buying or selling.

That's why the Sphere of Support campaign can be so powerful. If they start thinking of you as their real estate agent, they become immunized against all that other agent marketing. They tune it out. They have no reason to call on a sign, or click on a website's lead form, or sign up with some random agent at an open house. They already have an agent. They have you.

Will you retain them all? Sadly, no. You'll win some, and you'll lose some. Some of them are also in other agents' networks. Some will get sucked in an online lead. Some will walk into an open house and fall in love with the agent there. Some will be the exception and never, ever move. It happens. That's why you need the Sphere to be as big as possible. It's a numbers game.

Anyway, that direct business is only one of the ways that the people in your Sphere can support you. After all, even if they're not moving, they might know someone who is.

Chapter 3

The Top 100 Referral System: Not All Heroes Wear a Cape

WHAT'S THE BEST RESTAURANT IN YOUR HOME TOWN?

Let's say I was coming to your area to take some clients to dinner. Do you have a place you'd recommend to me?

Of course you do! Everyone has a favorite restaurant. And you'd probably leap at the chance to tell me about the place: what it's like, why I should go there, what I should order, and all that.

Why? Why are you so ready to refer me to that restaurant?

Are you getting a referral fee for every customer you send? Probably not.

Do you have an ownership stake? Probably not.

Am I paying you a fee for the referral? Most certainly not—I'm cheap!

No, it's not about a financial benefit. So why are you so eager to help me out?

It's simple: because everyone loves giving referrals. We just love it. We can't get enough of it.

Isn't that right? Don't you love making recommendations to your friends and colleagues? I'm not even talking about the professional referrals you might make for lenders, lawyers, and other people involved in your business, where you might have some indirect interest in supporting their practices.

No, I'm talking about purely selfless expressions of personal opinion. Watch this TV show. Eat at this restaurant. See this movie. Go to my dentist.

It goes on and on. We love sharing our opinion, guiding people to the stuff we love.

Indeed, companies have built huge businesses based primarily on the principle that people love sharing their opinions. We get nothing for it, and yet we'll take the time to compose exhaustive reviews of everything: books on Amazon, restaurants on Yelp, hotels on TripAdvisor, movies on Rotten Tomatoes, and so on. Essentially, we all work for free, providing enormously valuable content to companies that then monetize our efforts. Today, you find user-generated rating content on every retail site and even on search engines like Google and Bing. And all these opinions, at least the positive ones, are basically referrals: "you're thinking of buying this product? Here's why I loved it."

And that impulse is even stronger if it's a face-to-face personal referral, like the restaurant you'd recommend to me. If someone asks me for a recommendation, I feel obligated to come up with something good, and I'm disappointed if I can't think of anything.

Why do we all love making referrals so much? Is it because we're all just a bunch of do-gooders trying to do nice things for other people? Okay, maybe that's you. You're probably a very nice person. But not me. I have a lot of selfish reasons why I love giving referrals:

- *I get validation.* If I love a restaurant, recommend it to you, and then you love it, then you've validated my tastes. You've reinforced my self-image as someone who knows good food!

- *I provide support.* If I really like my hair stylist, I want her to do well—partly because I want to support her, but mostly so she doesn't go out of business and leave me with a grey head of unkempt hair!

- *I impress you.* If I refer you to someone, and you have a great experience, then you think more of me: "Wow! That Joe Rand really knows his foot doctors!"

- *You owe me!* If I refer you to a business, and you have a good experience, then I've earned a chit with you. I hooked you up, now it's your turn!

Indeed, the easiest way to sum up our internal incentives for making referrals is this: we want to be heroes. If you refer me to that restaurant, and I have a good experience, you're my hero. I think more highly of you, and I owe you.

But it's even better than that, because you could also be a hero to the restaurant owner! After all, isn't it possible that I might mention to the host or hostess how I heard about the place? So now you're not just a hero to me for referring me to a great restaurant, you're a hero to the restaurant for sending them a customer! A double-hero!

So with all that in mind, I have to ask: why are so many real estate agents denying all the people in their lives the glorious joys of being a double-hero?

"I KNEW YOU'D LOVE THAT PLUMBER, LOIS."

The Challenge of Building a Referral Base

Most real estate agents don't get enough personal referrals. Even great real estate agents, who do a lot of business through personal referrals, don't get enough of them.

Why is that? Great doctors, great lawyers, great electricians, great plumbers—most great service professionals build their practices through a dependable base of referral business without even having to work at it. Maybe a few of them join a BNI or some other network that aggressively manufactures referral opportunities, but most of them do little more than basic brand marketing. They don't even have dedicated salespeople. They just get a consistent stream of business from referrals from all their happy customers and clients.

So why do great real estate agents have to work so hard to get personal referrals? Why are we going to encourage you to send mailings, and make phone calls, and do all sorts of other stuff to cultivate a referral base? Why do we even need a whole chapter on how to build a referral base, when other professionals don't need to do any of that?

Here's the problem: not enough consumers look for real estate agents by referral, because they think that we're all the same. People ask around for referrals when they need someone to do work that they think is complicated, where expertise is important. You need a new doctor, you're going to ask your friends, or post a question on Facebook, because you know that there's a big difference between a good one and a bad one. Same for a lawyer, or architect, or electrician, or really any other service professional, whether white- or blue-collar. The more expertise required, the more likely you are to try to find someone by referral.

But too many people think that real estate agents are simply salespeople—and who looks for a referral for a salesperson? No one buying a car says to themselves, "I really should ask my friends who they used, because I want a really great car salesman!"

And that perception, that "Original Sin," feeds the misconception that all real estate agents are the same, and that the work we do does not require specific expertise. If a seller thinks that all an agent has to do is put a sign on the yard and throw an ad up on Zillow, then why does she need a great agent? And if a buyer thinks that she's probably going to find the home herself online, and that she only needs an agent for a lockbox key, then why spend a lot of time trying to find the right one? Might as well just work with whoever responds to that click on the website, or the agent who happens to be on up-time.

Now, we know that this is all untrue, that managing a real estate transaction requires significant expertise, and a great agent can make a huge difference for her clients. But it's still the perception that's out there, and it's a big challenge toward building a referral business.

Of course, even with this uphill battle against perception, it's not impossible to cultivate a referral business. In fact, that's exactly what great agents do: provide amazing experiences, make clients happy, and earn an outstanding reputation that separates them from the rest of the agents in the market. But it takes years and years for them to overcome the perception that all real estate agents are the same. They have to do great work for a lot of clients over a long time to earn that kind of word of mouth.

So is that it? Should we just close down this chapter?

Hey, it's too bad that you can't build a dependable referral base unless you've been doing great work for, say, 10-15 years. So go out, do great work, and it'll happen for you in about a decade. See you then! Now, let's talk about prospecting FSBOs!

No, we're not just going to write off one of the best ways to grow your business. We don't need to, because you can in fact accelerate the process of building that kind of reputation—one that will help you develop a dependable referral database. But you'll have to do more than doctors, or plumbers, or electricians have to do to develop their referral business. You'll have to spend time, and money, and energy. You'll have to work at it.

Unfortunately, most agents don't work at it. They'll put "I love referrals!" on their business card, or their website, or their email signature. They'll go to a seminar on generating referrals, and spend a few weeks sending out personal notes that they hope will spark some magic. Or they'll sign up for some expensive generic newsletter that gives their Sphere clients advice about gardening.

But they won't actually do the consistent, dedicated work it takes to cultivate a group of people into an evangelical referral base. You need a real Service-and-Marketing campaign. You need to aggressively reach out to your referral base with phone calls, texts, notes, mailings, and all sorts of personal touches.

Most of all, though, you need to be great at your job. Because if you're not great at your job, if you don't take excellent care of the buyers and sellers who trust you with their transaction, you're never going to get referral business. Your past clients will never want to inflict you on their friends and family, since you burned them on their own transaction. And your middling reputation will precede you, so that even your own family and friends won't want to risk recommending you.

Remember that people love giving referrals because they want to be heroes (even double-heroes!). They only refer the professionals they trust will make them look good. So they're not going to send you their best friend if they worry you're going to do a lousy job finding her a home. That doesn't make them look good, it makes them look terrible. They're not going to be a hero, they're going to be a fool.

So if you're not great at your job, then don't even bother trying to build a referral database. It's pointless. It doesn't matter how many mailings you send, or how many times you call, you're never going to get anything out of it.

But if you're willing to commit to being great at your actual job of giving your buyers and sellers amazing service experiences, then you would be foolish not to leverage that quality work, and the resulting reputation that you'll earn, into cultivating a referral database.

So how do you do it? We're going to take you through a three-part process:

1. Create a dedicated referral database within your Sphere of Support.

2. Implement a personal, high-touch Service-and-Marketing program designed to generate referrals.

3. Assertively reach out to your clients to ask for their support.

This will all take time, and a lot of work, but in the end it's worth it, because a stream of steady referrals can be a base of business for the rest of your career.

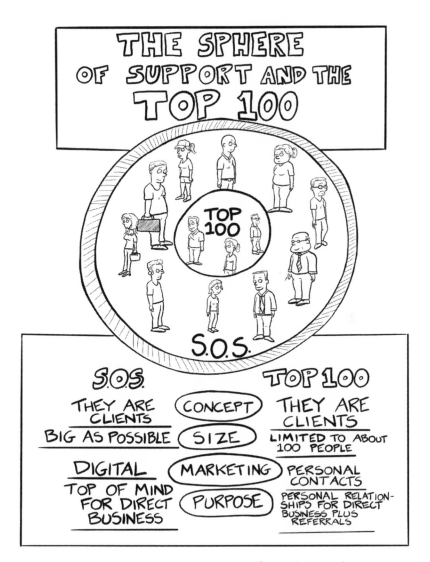

1. Building the Top 100: The Referral Database

We spent the last chapter encouraging you to make your Sphere of Support as big as possible.

Now, we want to go small.

Do you remember when you learned about Venn Diagrams in elementary school? Well, imagine the Sphere of Support as a big circle consisting of everyone you want to think of as a client, and everyone you want thinking of you as their real estate agent. You start with everyone you know, and then add everyone you meet, because the Sphere is scalable. You're going to provide your Courtesy Services through digital marketing, things like email newsletters.

But the general Sphere of Support campaign is not designed to generate personal referrals. If you want to cultivate a referral database, you need to spend a lot more time, energy, and money building personal relationships. You can't just click a few buttons, send out your digital marketing, and expect to activate people in your Sphere to send you referrals. You need a much more high-touch personal campaign that positions you as a more prominent and positive presence in their lives.

So within that big Sphere, we're going to create a much smaller circle, consisting of about 100 people, which we're going to call your "Top 100." You're going to pick out the very best people from your Sphere and give them an even higher level of attention and service in order to cultivate them into a consistent, predictable source of personal referrals. But that's going to require more than just digital marketing. You'll need to give them a lot more personal attention: phone calls and texts, physical mailings, gifts, personal notes and birthday cards, networking parties, and things like that. That's a lot of work, which is why you can't do it for everyone in your Sphere. Rather, you need to keep the Top 100 limited to, say, about 100 people. See how that works?

Who goes into your Top 100? These are your very best Sphere clients: not just all the people you know, but the people (1) you know and like the best, (2) who know and like you the best, and (3) are in the best position to refer you business.

Let's break that down:

1. *People you know and like the best.* These are the people closest to you: the family you still talk to, the friends that you see even outside of Facebook, your past clients, the neighbors you're not feuding with, and so on. Remember that your Sphere contains everyone you know even a little, but your Top 100 consists of people you know and also like.

2. *Who know and like you the best.* Even better, you think they like you, too! After all, they're not going to refer you business if they don't like you. When I started this program

at my own company, I had a half-dozen agents put a local mayor in their Top 100, because they thought he was so connected that he'd be a great referral source. And he would have been, except that none of them had a personal relationship with him. He didn't know any of them at all. He didn't belong in their Top 100.

3. *Who are in a position to refer you.* You might have a close friend, who knows and loves you immensely, but maybe they're not in the right position to refer you any potential business. What if you're their only friend, and they hate everyone else? Who are they going to refer to you? Or maybe they're lovely, but they don't have the kind of assertive personality where they'd enthusiastically recommend you to others. If they're not the type of person to send referrals, they probably don't belong in the Top 100.

The Top 100 is basically a subset of the overall Sphere: everyone who is in the Top 100 is part of the Sphere, but not everyone in the Sphere is in the Top 100. But the conceptual relationship is the same. They're all your clients. You're the real estate agent for all of them. The only difference is the type of Service-and-Marketing program you provide to them.

Indeed, the nexus between the Sphere and the Top 100 is crucial to solving one of the biggest problems with the traditional Sphere of Influence: how do you continue to cultivate those personal relationships when your Sphere expands over the course of your career?

For example, let's say that you started your career with 100 people in a traditional Sphere of Influence. Easy enough to call and mail to 100 people every month or so. But now you're actively in the business, and you're out there meeting new people like that florist, people you'd like to add to your Sphere. And if you're good at your job, you're selling houses, which means that you're generating new "past clients" every month. So your Sphere gets bigger.

But now you have a problem: you can't possibly afford the time or money it will take to keep cultivating this growing group. Once you get up to 150-200 people, or more, you're going to stretch yourself too thin. You don't have the time to make personal connections, and you don't have the money to keep up with the mailings.

So what do you do? You have to cut people. That's the traditional system: as you add people, you have to cut others. Organize the people in your Sphere into tiers, and delete those who aren't making the cut. Get rid of them if they don't pick up the phone when you call, or seem unenthusiastic when you talk, or, even worse, never send you referrals.

Now, think about that. For the last few years, you've been sending your monthly mailings to these people and calling them periodically. Now, you cut them off. No more calls. No more mailings. They're out.

Don't you think they notice that? Don't you think they wonder why you stopped paying attention to them? And isn't it likely that, instead of realizing that they weren't performing up to your expectations, they're going to think that you're just another inconsistent real estate agent who can't keep up a program?

That's not being very client-oriented. That's not thinking about what people need, it's about thinking about what we need. That's what the traditional Sphere of Influence forced you to do: cut people out of your life if they didn't perform to your expectations.

But the inter-relationship between the Sphere of Support and the Top 100 solves that problem. When you take people out of your Top 100, they go right into the general Sphere. They're still clients, getting the digital marketing campaign. And hopefully they still think of you as their agent and will still come to you when they need to buy or sell a home. The only difference is that you're no longer going to expect referrals from them, because, although you're staying in their lives, you're not going to be giving them the kind of personal attention that drives referrals.

2. The Top 100 Service-and-Marketing Program

Right now, at this very moment, you are one degree of separation from hundreds of people who are in the process of moving.

Here's what I mean. According to studies of personal networks, the average person knows about 300 people well. So with apologies to those of you who were told there would be no math, let's run those numbers: the 100 people in your Top 100 put you at one degree of separation away from about 30,000 people (100 x 300 = 30,000). And at any given time, studies show that about 3% of those people are going to be in the process of looking to buy or sell a home. Add it all up: collectively, the people in your Top 100 right now know about 900 people (3% of 30,000) who are going to move this year.

So why aren't you getting any of those referrals? Because the topic never comes up. Your Top 100 clients don't know the people are moving. And, even if it does come up, even if those people happen to mention that they're thinking of putting their home on the market, your Top 100 clients aren't attuned to notice it. It just passes right by them. Opportunity lost.

That's the purpose of the Top 100 Service-and-Marketing program: to activate them to think and talk about real estate, so that they get into the kinds of conversations that will lead to referrals. The more you inform and educate them, the more likely they are to find themselves in conversations about real estate, which will lead to situations to refer you.

So what goes into the campaign? Well, it starts with a foundational mailing program, which you can then supplement with any number of personal touches, including a yearly CMA, birthday cards, social media engagement, gifts, and even networking parties

Mailing Campaign. Just like with the Sphere, the foundation for your Top 100 campaign should be some sort of regular mailing that hits on the three CORE Courtesy Services: information about the market, property management, and the community. That's your expertise. That's what you want to activate people to think about. The difference, of course, is that the Sphere campaign is purely digital, while the Top 100 campaign is going to require physical, tangible pieces.

So yes, this is going to cost some time and money, more than the minimal amount that you might spend for your digital marketing. You need envelopes, and stamps, and physical pieces that look beautiful. And you need the time to stuff those envelopes and send them out. But these investments are worth it, because you want to send a message to the people in your Top 100 that you're taking personal care of them. You didn't just tap three buttons and shoot them a digital piece. You took the time to lick a stamp, and stuff an envelope, and you spent some money on them.

Courtesy CMA. Create a short CMA for everyone in your Top 100, once a year. After all, agents have always been willing to give a "Free CMA!" to any random schlub who calls on their ad, so why not give one every year to the most important people in your business—your referral sources?

Maybe it seems quaint today, this idea of sending out a simple Courtesy CMA at a time when your clients can just go online and get an automated valuation like a Zestimate that gives them an actual estimate of their property value. But I think it still has value. I think people still like to get a report that tells them what's selling and what's sold in their local markets, especially one that comes from a professional real estate agent who knows that market better than any online system. Most homeowners can never get enough information relating to the value of their home. They will open it, they will read it, they will appreciate it, and they will remember this amazing service you provided them.

Birthday Card. Send everyone in your Top 100 a birthday card every year. You don't need anything fancy or expensive, just a simple notecard that says, "Happy Birthday," with space where you can add a personal hand-written message.

Maybe this also seems quaint, this idea of sending a birthday card when people already get hundreds of "HBD!" messages on their Facebook wall or their email. But that's the point—a personal, hand-written birthday card stands out, precisely because no one sends them anymore. It takes all of two minutes, but it sends a personal, intimate message to that client: I was thinking about you, and I took the time to remember your birthday.

Seriously, how many actual birthday cards did you get last year? Exactly!

The birthday card is an important part of the Top 100 marketing campaign, because it warms up a program that is otherwise so coolly professional, designed to enforce your traditional role as a real estate agent. The card is a personal gesture amid a cascade of professional pieces. Even better, it's automatic. You don't have to get creative, or think too hard, you just need to follow your schedule and send it out once a year.

Social Media Engagement. Let me start by saying that you don't have to use social media for your business. It's fine if you want to, say, keep Facebook limited to your friends and personal use. That's fine. But if you do use social media for business, then you should be engaging with the people in your Top 100.

Most agents, unfortunately, get social media all wrong. They spend all their time broadcasting, rather than listening. You should spend about 90% of your time on social media paying attention to what other people post, rather than posting something of your own. Scan your feed, and like and comment on everything you see: like, like, like, like, comment, like, comment, like, like, like, comment. On and on.

Yes, of course you should also post regularly, but the key to engaging with other people—whether on social media or in person—is to pay attention to them. Listen to them. Show an authentic interest in them. That's how you build rapport, and that's how you engage. People notice when you like the photos of their kids, or the articles they post, and they appreciate it.

So scan your feed every day looking for interesting posts from the people in your Top 100. That means, of course, you should friend all the people in your Top 100. If they're not willing to accept a friend request, that's a pretty good sign that you need to screen your database a little better.

Gifts. If you get a referral from someone in your Top 100 (or anyone, really), you need to send them a thank-you gift. Right away. The minute you get the referral. You don't wait until you make contact, you don't wait until you get the listing, you don't wait until the closing. No, you send the gift the day that person gives you the referral.

Why? Because it's not their job to make contact, or get you the listing, or sell the house. That's your job. Their job was just to think of you, and to connect you to the referral. They did their job. So thank them with a gift.

One of the reasons the Top 100 program works is the concept of reciprocity, the cognitive impulse to return favors. You get, and then you give. Our brains are hard-wired to reciprocate favors, going back to the cave-dwelling days when "you scratch my back, I scratch yours" had the literal meaning of picking out, you know, fleas and ticks. We've evolved since then, most of us, but we still feel compelled to reciprocate when someone does us a favor. They invite us to dinner, we have to have them over in return. They send us a holiday card, we have to send them one. We need things to be even-steven like that.

And that's why you send a thank-you gift. You did a favor by providing Courtesy Services, the Top 100 client reciprocated by sending you a referral, now you reciprocate back by sending them a gift. Which means it's their turn again!

Networking Parties. I've never really loved the concept of the "Client Appreciation Party"—agents throwing a party for their referral clients to thank them for their support. It's a nice idea, and I understand the impulse, but I guess I'm leery of throwing a party that's so explicitly focused on the agent, rather than the client. And I'm just not sure how excited I'd be about going to a party with a bunch of people I probably don't know, who I'm only connected to because, say, we have the same accountant.

That's why I recommend instead a "Networking Party," a party that's not about you, but about them—the people in your Top 100. Focus on their needs, not yours. After all, most of them are probably professionals in their own right, maybe even entrepreneurs, and they generally welcome opportunities to network with potential clients.

So why not throw one for them? Go to a local restaurant with a bar, find out what their slowest weeknight time is, and then tell them you'll bring a few dozen people if they'll give you a break on the drink prices, and throw in some apps. Then book it for an hour or two of open bar. You won't end up spending all that much on alcohol, because (most) people drink less in a professional setting like a networking party. Put it this way: if you run up a huge bar bill, that's a sign that you have a bigger problem—too many drunks in your life.

The key is: the party is about them, not you. Yes, at some point you clink glasses and make a short speech thanking them for all the support they've given you, but the focus of the event is to make the effort to connect them professionally. And at the very least, you send a sub-textual message: I care about helping you build your business, the way you care about helping me build mine.

3. A Reason to Call

The Top 100 Service-and-Marketing program is the foundation for the referral system. The mailing program positions you as their real estate agent, provides a nice service, and activates them to think and talk about real estate. And the rest of the campaign—the CMA, birthday card, social media attention, gifts, and parties—helps build that relationship, embracing both your professional obligations and your personal connections.

But none of these things generates referrals. You can only really get consistent referrals one way: making phone calls. Indeed, you should think of everything else you do—the mailings, the birthday cards, the gifts, everything—as just a "reason to call."

I know, I know—phone calls! Agents hate making phone calls, even to the people they know and like, because they think they're taking advantage of people. But think of it this way: as a call from your doctor. Do you mind when you get a follow-up call from your doctor, or lawyer, or dentist, or financial planner, or anyone else that you do business with? Generally, you don't mind those kinds of calls. In fact, you're probably happy when you get them, grateful that the doctor or lawyer or whoever reached out to you personally to give you information.

Why? Because you perceived that call as a service, not a solicitation. Even if the call is designed to maintain or cultivate the professional relationship you've developed, you still don't resent the call.

That's the attitude that you need to make when you're reaching out to people. Stop thinking like a salesperson, and start thinking about the service you can provide to whomever you're calling. Why are you calling? Well, as we just said, most of the Top 100 campaign is designed to give you good reasons to call:

Hi Bob, it's Joe, I only have a few moments, but I wanted to call because:

- *I wanted to see if you had any questions about the market report I just sent...*

- *I wanted you to be on the lookout for our latest market report...*

- *I was wondering if you might know of any fun community events for our upcoming seasonal guide...*

- *I wanted to wish you a happy birthday...*

- *I wanted to go over the Courtesy CMA I emailed last week...*

- *I wanted to see if you're coming to our networking party...*

- *I saw the great news on Facebook, and wanted to congratulate you personally...*

- *I thought you might be curious what that home down your block sold for....*

In other words, if you're firing off on all the other parts of the Service-and-Marketing campaign, you always have a reason to call. Either you just sent them something and want to go over it, or you're about to send something and want them to be on the lookout for it. At the very least, you can start a conversation and see where it leads.

And, of course, when you finish, always end by asking them to think of someone they might be able to refer to you:

Bob, while I have you on the phone, who do you know that might be able to use my services? Any of your friends, family, people from work, your neighborhood? I promise to take great care of them.

You see how that conversation goes? It's not so bad, right?

So make the call. The personal phone call to the people in your Top 100 is the most important part of the program:

First, that phone call is the single best way to generate a referral. No matter how much your clients like you, no matter how much they would be willing to refer you if given the opportunity, they need to be regularly reminded that you're available to them or anyone they know. You'd be amazed at how often they'll only come up with a name if you ask them point-blank. Yes, you'll occasionally get a call or email out of the blue with a referral opportunity, but most of them will come from assertively reaching out yourself.

Second, the phone call is part of the great service you provide to your Top 100. The call gives them the opportunity to ask you questions about the market, or your opportunity to go over the mailing you just sent them. More importantly, they might have something else that you can help them with. Maybe they're thinking of putting in that new kitchen and want your opinion, or they're curious about the new business opening up in town. They might not want to bother you, so they're not going to call you. But if you call them, they'll open up to you.

Third, the phone call is crucial to helping you screen your Top 100. Remember that your Top 100 is a living database: people come in, people come out. The only way to do that is to make sure you're talking to your people. As time goes by, you'll get a feel for who is most likely to refer you, and who should be dropped down to the

Sphere. In our experience, very few Top 100 clients have a bad reaction to the phone call. But even if you do sometimes call someone you thought would be supportive, only to find them getting angry at you or hanging up, that's actually a good thing. Why? Because you can just take that person off your Top 100 and stop wasting time and resources on them. That makes your database stronger, opening up a spot for someone who might be more supportive. The negative vibe lasts for a few seconds, but the improvement to your Top 100 enriches you for the rest of your career.

So make the call!

Or, alternatively, send the text!

We all know that some of your clients, particularly the younger ones, rarely talk on the phone. That's fine. Today, texting is the equivalent of calling. For our purposes, calling is better, because actually talking to someone on the phone is more personal and intimate. But if you have a Top 100 client who never picks up the phone when you call, texting is the next best thing.

Follow the same system: find a reason to text people, send them a message that plays off something you've sent or are sending them. For example:

Hi John, it's Joe, didn't want to bother you with a call, but wanted to see if you got the market report I sent. Feel free to get back to me if you have any questions.

If you send a text like that, you'll either get: (1) some kind of engagement, which can lead to a textual discussion of whether they know anyone who might be moving, (2) a simple acknowledgement, which will cut off the conversation, but at least you've made a soft touch, or (3) no response, which is not good, but it helps you screen your database if your Top 100 client consistently blows you off.

Your Service-and-Marketing campaign is designed to accommodate the needs of your clients. If they don't like talking on the phone, then adjust to them.

Because, never forget, it's always about them, not you.

Chapter 4

From Old to SOLD:
The Bottle of Wine

NEVER SHOW UP EMPTY-HANDED.

Right? Someone invites you over to their home for a party or a dinner or something, and you bring a bottle of wine. Or some flowers. Or a cake.

Whatever. You bring something. Anything. You don't show up at someone's house with nothing but a knife and a fork clutched in your grubby little hands.

We all learn this as little kids. I can remember my Italian grandmother teaching me that if you visit someone in their home, you bring something with you as a sign of respect and to thank them for inviting you. She was Italian, so the "something" was usually pretty tasty food. She explained that it was an "Italian tradition."

Around the same time, my Irish grandmother told me basically the same thing, that when you go to someone's house, you bring them something. She was Irish, so that "something" was often a bottle. And she explained it as an "Irish tradition."

I've since come to learn that it's a tradition for pretty much every culture. Italian. Irish. English. French. Spanish. Chinese. Russian. Japanese. Jewish. All of them. And it could be a bottle, or a dish, or flowers, or pretty much anything. But no one in the world teaches you that it's okay to show up at someone's house for a party with nothing but your appetite.

And yet, that's what real estate agents do every day when they try to generate business. They essentially show up at someone's house empty-handed, with nothing to offer except a knife and fork.

"KNIFE AND FORK PROSPECTING"

Here's what I mean: let's take a look at a classic prospecting script:

Hi, this is Joe Rand from Basement Realty, and I'm calling because we recently sold a home in your neighborhood, and we know that when someone sells a home, usually two more sell right away. So I was wondering—when do you plan on moving?

"When do you plan on moving?" Such a classic question, and a powerful one. Why? Because like most prospecting scripts, it doesn't allow for a "yes" or "no" answer. Rather, it provokes the homeowner to reflexively think for a moment about when they actually plan on moving. If their answer indicates they're thinking of moving anytime soon, then you start closing for an appointment.

Here's the problem: these days, most of the time, they don't answer the question. They didn't pick up the phone, because their caller ID squealed on you, letting the homeowner know that you're a real estate agent. Even if they did pick up the phone, they hung up on you halfway through your script, because most people hate telemarketing. Or maybe you couldn't even make that call, because everyone in the neighborhood is on the "Do-Not-Call-List," the script is clearly a restricted solicitation, and you don't think you'd do very well in jail.

But the biggest reason that traditional prospecting doesn't really work is that, well, you don't actually do it. Yes, you probably tried at some point in your career. You went to a conference and got all fired up by a guru who preached about how easy it is if you're just willing to apply yourself to make two or three hours of calls a day. "Just keep calling until you get an appointment!" Sounds so easy!

So you plunked down your credit card to buy those scripts and tapes and promised yourself that this time you were going to stick with it. Then you went back to the office, pinned up those scripts on your wall, put up a dream board or something like that, and started making calls.

For about half an hour.

Then, after realizing that a soul-sucking regimen of cold-calling people to manipulate them into setting an appointment was not for you, you put those scripts and tapes back in a drawer.

And never were they seen again!

You're not alone. Most people can't stomach a regimen of traditional cold call prospecting. Why? Because it makes you feel bad about yourself. It's selfish, and manipulative, and focused entirely on your own needs. It's like showing up at someone's house with nothing but your knife and fork.

What are you bringing to the party when you call someone with a "when do you plan on moving" script? Are you providing them with anything useful—information that they might find valuable? If anything, you're lying to them, with some made-up nonsense about how "when one home sells, others soon follow!" You're not calling to do anything for them, you're just calling to see whether they can do anything for you. It's not a good feeling.

And it's not just the "Just Listed" script. Traditional prospecting is all about the needs of the agent—the need for a listing, or a deal—with the complete disregard for the needs of the client:

- *You just scheduled an open house?* Call around the neighborhood to see if they know anyone who might want to move to the area and when they plan on moving!

- *Someone is selling their house on their own?* Okay, call her and ask, "How long are you going to wait until you hire a professional agent to handle your sale?"

- *Someone's listing expired?* Call her to tell her how many homes you've sold since hers went on the market, and ask, "How long until you go back on the market?"

Traditional prospecting is never about how the agent can help the client; only about how the client can help the agent: send me a buyer, interview me for the job, list with me.

We don't have to do things that way. What would happen if we flipped that mindset, elevating the needs of the client over the needs of the agent? What if we generated business by following the CORE Formula and thought creatively about how we can service people's needs, which might help establish a relationship with them?

In other words, what if we showed up to the party with a bottle of wine?

(Metaphorically, I mean. Don't literally go door-knock a FSBO seller with a bottle of wine in your hand.)

(Although, frankly, it couldn't hurt.)

(No, seriously, don't do that.)

Think about how focusing on the needs of the potential client changes the traditional lead generation dynamic:

- *You just scheduled an open house?* Call the neighbors as a courtesy to notify them so that they don't get concerned if they see some unfamiliar cars on the street, and trust that if they're at all interested in real estate right now, they're going to engage you in a conversation about the particulars of your new listing.

- *Someone is selling a house on their own?* That's really hard to do! Who knows better than you how tough it is to sell a home? Perhaps she could use some sort of comparative market analysis to help price her home, so maybe you should drop one off, and then follow up to see if she has any questions.

- *Someone's listing expired?* Wow, she's probably really curious as to why her home didn't sell. Maybe she would appreciate an analysis of why listings expire, along with a way to evaluate where she stands in the market, with a follow-up phone call to see if she got it.

The goal is the same: make a connection to the person selling her home, or the neighbors for your new listing. But the process is completely different. Rather than reaching out to them for the purpose of trying to generate a piece of business, you're now trying to provide them a service, purely as a courtesy to them.

That's the essence of what we call "Service-Oriented Lead Development," or SOLD, because we're all about the silly acronyms here at CORE headquarters! Build your business by thinking expansively about what people need, and then creatively about how to give it to them.

SOLD changes the traditional lead generation mindset. It's not about what people can do for you, it's about what you can do for them. We've already seen how this approach changes the dynamic with the people in your Top 100: you reach out to them to see if they got your market report, or your event guide, not just to see whether they know anyone who is buying or selling.

Think of how we followed this "bottle of wine" approach in the Top 100. Calling your past clients with nothing more than a "who do you know that's selling?" dialogue is no way to build the kind of meaningful connection that leads to personal referrals. But if you've been sending them helpful information about what's going on in the market and the community, you've earned the right to reach out to them. Why? Because you brought something of value to the exchange.

More importantly, SOLD is a campaign you can actually follow, not try once and then put back in that drawer. You won't feel like you're using people if you make the kind of calls we want you to make. You won't feel bad about yourself, and you won't feel self-conscious about your motivations. Essentially, you earn the right to reach out to your potential clients by providing services to them. You'll feel more confident and justified in reaching out to a FSBO seller if you've already dropped off a CMA. Why? Because you brought a (metaphorical!) bottle of wine to the party.

And that mindset is important. SOLD basically gives you that "reason to call"—a purpose for reaching out to people beyond your own self-interest. And that reason to call is what's so important, because if you can convince yourself that you're doing something for that person's benefit, not just your own, you're much more likely to make the call in the first place.

Essentially, SOLD relies on what we'll call a "dual-motivation": first, the altruistic motivation of being great at your job, expanding your perception of what people need and thinking creatively about the services you can provide to them; and second, the self-interested incentive of establishing relationships that can lead to business opportunities.

And that's okay! You can want both those things at the same time without being a manipulative user. In fact, these types of dual motivations make the world go 'round. I've joined nonprofit boards not just because I believe in the cause, but because I think it will help me meet new clients. I give money to charity not just because I want to give back but because I want to be included in the annual report and raise my company's profile. When I was single, I would buy women drinks at bars, not because I was a generous person but because that was the only way to get them to talk to me for even a minute.

Dual motivations! Most people need at least some sort of incentive to do good things. Maybe not Mother Theresa, but the rest of us do.

Face it. Most agents are their own worst enemy. Their biggest obstacle to doing consistently effective lead generation is between their ears: the self-consciousness they feel about contacting other people to ask for business. But if we can eliminate that discomfiting feeling, we can break through that roadblock. And focusing on your selfless motivation—the motivation to provide services to people— makes it easier to pick up that phone. If you have a reason to call, other than the fact that you want business, you're more likely to make that call.

And you do need to make the call! We don't teach SOLD to help you be a "not-for-profit" real estate agent. It's not about sitting around a campfire singing "Kumbaya" and giving away free stuff to people just to generate good karma. You still have to make calls to people you know, and the ones you don't know. But because those calls can sometimes be uncomfortable, SOLD tries to make it easier.

I'm not saying that the SOLD way is easy. It's not. It takes a lot of work, and you'll often have to come out of your comfort zone. You're not going to sit around waiting for business to come to you. You'll invest a lot of time, a lot of effort, and even some money.

And as you'll see, the mechanics of SOLD are basically the same as traditional prospecting. We still want you to hold open houses, conduct personal marketing, build a farm, and solicit unrepresented sellers (i.e., FSBOs and Expireds). We haven't invented a new source of business; we've created a new mindset for generating opportunities from old sources of business.

But it's a better way to grow your career than through traditional prospecting. It's a program you can feel good about, even proud of, because your focus is on serving other people's needs. In fact, you can take this book, open it to any page, and show it to your clients—"this is what I'm doing to improve my business."

Could you do that with most real estate training books?

Courtesy Calls

You need to make phone calls. I'm sorry to tell you that, but it's true. You will never find a better way to generate potential business opportunities than actually talking to people on the phone.

But you don't need to make *cold* calls. I'm not a believer in making cold calls. It's not just that most agents won't actually make them, since they suck the soul from your body and leave you a dry, desiccated zombie. It's more that cold calls don't really work anymore, at least not as well as they used to, because consumers have evolved. They're now wise to those types of solicitations, and have learned how to avoid us at our most annoying. When the gurus who encourage you to make cold calls started in the business, people didn't have the same skepticism for solicitations that they have today: they listed their phone numbers, answered their phones, and even set up voicemail so they wouldn't miss a call.

But times have changed. Now, they un-list their number, ignore the rings, and use voicemail so they never have to actually talk to anyone. Yes, cold calling still works, through the sheer blunt force of making call after call after call long enough to find someone who's thinking of selling. But it's an incredibly inefficient way to generate business.

I do, though, believe in making calls. I just think you need to find a reason to call, a service-oriented purpose that warms that cold call up into something that's at least not going to cause too much metaphorical shrinkage.

Which brings us to the "Courtesy Call." We've used the word "courtesy" before to refer to services that we provide for free to the people in our Sphere and Top 100, keeping them informed about the market, their property, and the community. Remember, the idea is that couching an act as a courtesy is a disarming way of providing a service to someone who might otherwise be resistant to your attempts to help them. Everyone loves getting something as a courtesy.

More importantly, thinking of the services you provide as a courtesy to others helps you embrace the mindset that your lead generation is all about doing something for other people, not for yourself. You're bringing that bottle of wine.

You can make all sorts of Courtesy Calls, but let's focus on the most common—the Just Listed Courtesy Call—to illustrate the system. Let's say that you just took a listing, and you'd like to make some "Just Listed" calls to see if you can find a neighbor thinking of moving, or at least someone you might add to your Sphere. The traditional Just Listed call is classic knife-and-fork:

We just listed a home in your area, and we know that when one home in a neighborhood comes on the market, two or three more soon follow. So when do you plan on moving?

Can we warm that up? Yes, but what we need is some sort of purpose, beyond the self-interested goal of finding out if that person is moving.

So let's think expansively about what these people in the neighborhood need? Think about what it's like when you live near a home that goes on the market. A sign goes up, basically a big distracting billboard on the middle of that otherwise quiet residential street. People pass by, slow down to read it, maybe take down a phone number as they're driving. On weekends, you might see more signs, the directional open house signs on all the corners, with big balloons hovering over them, directing people driving unfamiliar roads while looking at the maps on their phones or dashboards. If the listing gets a lot of showings, you're constantly seeing strangers coming in and out of your neighborhood, looking things over, sometimes parking in front of your house.

It's actually really annoying. If a nearby house goes on the market, it's a distraction, and a disturbance. It might even be dangerous if you have young kids that like to play on the street, what with all these buyers driving around lost looking their map while they yap it up with their agent about bedrooms and bathrooms.

Put it this way: if you were throwing a big family reunion at your home that was going to bring a lot of people to your block who were going to be parking all over the place and causing a disturbance, wouldn't you call the neighbors to let them know? Just as, oh I don't know, a courtesy?

That's the mindset. You just took a listing in that neighborhood. As a courtesy, you should call everyone on the block to let them know that you're going to be putting up a sign, and listing the address online, and bringing a whole bunch of visitors to broker and public open houses, and otherwise making a real nuisance of yourself.

Now, I know that it's not the most crucial of services, this idea that you're going to warn the neighborhood that you're about to take a nearby listing. You might even argue that it's a pretext. But if you can just convince yourself, get into your own mind, that you're making that call because you're trying to provide a service, even a minor one, you'll find it easier to make the call. And if you can make the call, you'll discover something interesting: people actually appreciate it. They like the courtesy of letting them know that a house in their area is coming on the market. Indeed, they'll actually thank you!

So get the permission of your sellers to call the people in the neighborhood, and then make the call:

Hi, is this the Smith residence? This is Joe Rand from Rand Realty, and your neighbors, the Millers, asked me to call you as a courtesy to let you know we're about to list their home at 123 Bluebird Lane. Just so you're warned that you might see some unfamiliar cars on the street or people coming in and out of the neighborhood. Okay? Great! And if you have any questions, feel free to call me at...

You'll notice that it doesn't include a solicitation. Don't ask them if they're thinking of selling, don't ask them if they know any buyers, don't ask them if they know anyone else in the neighborhood who is moving. You're calling to provide them with a service, to notify them that a home in their area is going on the market. If you make a solicitation, you're violating the spirit in which you called them.

Even worse, if you make a solicitation, your call might be a violation of the Do-Not-Call-List. The Courtesy Call is not a solicitation, so it's (arguably—I'm a lawyer, but I'm not *your* lawyer) not covered by the national Do-Not-Call Registry. You're not calling to solicit business, you're calling on behalf of the sellers to warn the neighbors that the home is going on the market. But if you throw in something like "when do you plan on moving?," you could be violating the law.

And you don't need to make that solicitation, because if that neighbor is at all interested in the market, he's going to ask you questions. And then once he's asking questions, you take the conversation wherever it leads. Indeed, the Courtesy Call sparks the exact kind of conversation about the real estate market that traditional scripts are designed to induce.

Of course, all this presupposes that someone answers the phone. That's not going to happen all the time, or even most of the time. People just don't pick up their home phone like they used to. Even if you get the neighbors' mobile phone numbers from your sellers (which you should ask for), you most likely won't get through. But that's okay. You can just leave that courtesy message on the voicemail. Not great, but better than nothing.

Essentially, the Courtesy Call warms up the traditional Just Listed cold call with a secondary purpose, a service you can provide that neighbor. That's your mindset, which makes it easier for you to actually make the call, and the one after that, and the one after that. And once you're on the phone with someone, anything can happen.

Indeed, it's not just about Just Listed calls. You can replace every call you might make in your business development work: open houses, lead follow-up, farming, FSBOs, Expireds. Never forget the magic of the word "courtesy," and warm up all your cold calls as Courtesy Calls.

Listing Marketing

The single best way to generate a lead in real estate is very simple: get a listing, and market it well.

Listings are the currency of real estate lead generation, because a well-marketed listing establishes a platform for a whole variety of effective lead development techniques:

- *Online Advertising.* A new listing is the basis for a whole suite of advertising tools that are the best and most cost-effective form of lead generation in the modern age: your own website or app, portal syndication, and search and social media advertising.

- *Print Advertising.* Since some sellers and buyers still look to print, you can market your listing through selected print channels, ideally specialized magazines or hyper-local community newspapers.

- *Mailings.* You can send a series of "just listed" cards, and eventually "just sold" cards, to either the neighborhood or a targeted buyer audience.

- *Open Houses.* You can take an active listing and invite the whole world to come visit.

- *Courtesy Calls.* And, of course, a new listing is a great reason to make Courtesy Calls to the neighborhood.

The key, of course, is not just to market the listing, but market it well. Why? Because your marketing is the best service you can provide for both your seller and your prospective buyer.

Indeed, listing marketing is a perfect articulation of the dual-purpose methodology of SOLD: it's good for our seller clients, and it's good for us. That should be your mindset. Think about the service that you're providing to your seller, rather than the more mercenary interest that you have in generating leads. If you think about your client's needs, rather than your own, you'll find it easier for you to do the hard, and sometimes discouraging, work of reaching out to people you don't know. You're not doing something for yourself when you're replying to online inquiries, or calling the neighborhood, or sending a mailing—you're doing quality work for your seller.

Even better, think also about how you can provide a great service to the people you're marketing to. Neighbors getting your Courtesy Calls and mailings are probably curious as to what's happening in the market, particularly in the local area, so service their needs by reaching out to them with information that they'll find helpful. Following up with online leads, particularly people who are tough to track down, is a chore, but they called you for a reason: they wanted to find out more about that home, so keep following up until you've answered their questions. You're always more likely to engage in lead generation activities if you focus on servicing their needs, rather than your own.

Essentially, great listing marketing serves not just two purposes, but three: it's good for you because it generates leads, it's good for sellers in helping to get their home sold, and it's good for buyers who want as much information as possible about homes for sale. It's not a dual-purpose, it's a tri-purpose!

Open Houses

Let's think about the client-oriented purpose of open houses, rather than just our own purpose to generate a potential lead. What's the bottle of wine?

Start with the buy-side. Open houses provide showing opportunities to very specific types of purchasers, those at an early stage of their home-buying process. While they're just idly thinking about buying, when it's just a glimmer of an idea, not yet a reality, they like to go to open houses to get a sense of the market. They know that they could always make an appointment to see the home at their convenience, but they don't want to commit to working with an agent. They worry they'll feel pressured when they're not ready yet, or they simply don't want to "bother" an agent with what is still a fanciful notion. They don't want to dive in, they just want to dip their toe. So they go to open houses.

That's the service we provide to buyers: a low-pressure, no-commitment way to acclimate to the idea of buying.

And what about sellers? What do they get out of opening their house to a bunch of people with no present intention to buy? Well, sometimes, those idle looky-loos fall in love with a home and become actual, real-life buyers. It happens! And sellers know that, which is why they don't need to be persuaded to hold an open house. They love open houses!

Indeed, they often have to harangue their tired, jaded agent to hold one. Have you ever tried to take a Sunday off by telling a seller that open houses don't work, that other agents just have them to generate leads? The conversations go kind of like that scene in *Dumb and Dumber*:

Seller: So what are my chances of selling through an open house?

Agent: Not good.

Seller: So not good like 1 out of a 100?

Agent: Um, more like 1 out of a million.

Seller: So... YOU'RE TELLING ME THERE'S A CHANCE!

Agent: [slapping hand to forehead.]

Seller: SEE YOU SUNDAY!

Here's the thing: why are you even trying to convince them not to do an open house? You have so many things you need to persuade your seller about: price, commission, staging, not blowing a deal up because they don't like what the buyer said about their drapes. Why try to fight their preconceptions about open houses? At the very least, an open house is a placebo, a vivid and tangible demonstration that you're working hard to sell the home.

On top of all that, open houses can be powerful lead generators, and a nice way to add people to your Sphere with the "Who Would You Call...?" dialogue. That is, we have that tri-purpose: they're good for buyers, good for sellers, and good for you.

At least, open houses can be tremendous lead generators if you do them correctly, with Courtesy Calls to the neighborhood, mailings, online advertising, and all that. And if you're going to do all that work to generate visitors to your open house, make sure you follow up. You need to call, email, and/or text everyone who came to your open house. After all, you have a strong reason to call: your seller asked you to get feedback from all the visitors. So make those calls, and then, while you're on the phone, you can be more assertive about probing their interest in buying, or, if you didn't get the chance at the open house, use the "Who Would You Call...?" dialogue.

Remember: follow-up isn't just about you, it's about your seller client. It's you being great at your job.

Geographic Farming

The whole idea of "farming" sounds horrible. Seriously. Have you ever seen a farmer? They never look happy. They're out in the fields all day, under a hot sun, digging away at the Earth. Not an easy life. Doesn't sound like a fun way to develop your business.

And it's really no better for your potential clients, right? I mean, what are they in this whole concept—the vegetables? No one wants to be a vegetable. You're stuck in the ground, bugs eat you, best case scenario is you end up boiled in some pot.

It's not just the metaphor—in reality, geographic farming is just about the hardest way real estate agents can generate business. Indeed, I don't think that agents should even try to build a farm until they're already developed a mature and flourishing Sphere of Support and are looking for new mountains to scale. If you still haven't developed your Sphere, don't even think about farming.

Why? Because a geographic farm is a wholly inferior version of the Sphere. It's the same basic concept: compile a list of people, market consistently to them for a long period of time, and try to position yourself as their real estate agent. But farms are just a lot harder, because the people in your farm don't know you like the people in your Sphere. That's why you have to invest a lot of money over a long period of time to get results. So trust me, if you haven't yet built up your Sphere, put your energies there. Anything your farm can do, your Sphere can do better, cheaper, and easier. And even if you've built the Sphere, you'll get much more bang for the buck if you focus your energies on cultivating your Top 100 into a consistent referral base.

But if you do have the bandwidth to cultivate a farm, you'll find it's similar to building your Sphere. After all, the people living in your farm are probably homeowners who have the same basic need for Courtesy Services that your Sphere does: information about the market, property management, and the community. And the goals are the same: provide services to satisfy those needs and position yourself as their real estate agent.

The difference from Sphere marketing, of course, is that we're going to have to provide those services mostly through mailings to a much larger group of people, which can be expensive. So you should try to leverage that costly ground game with some cheaper air support: digital assets that reinforce your position as the go-to real estate agent for that community. You can create a whole series of online resources that will cost you almost nothing, require very little maintenance, and create the impression that you are the leading expert for that neighborhood:

- *Facebook Groups.* A few years ago, I created a Facebook group for my hometown called "We Love Nyack," as an open forum for discussions, announcements, reviews, and anything else about the Village. It wasn't about me. It wasn't about my company. It was about Nyack, and all the reasons why it was such a wonderful place to live. How much did this cost me? Literally, nothing. You can do the exact same thing for a local community: create a discussion group, write posts about the neighborhood, share them through your personal feed, and invite anyone you know to join the group.

- *Pinterest.* Create a Pinterest board dedicated to beautiful photography of the neighborhood. Take a bunch yourself but search online for photos from other people that you can feature and link to. Give it an SEO-friendly title and spend five minutes a week updating it.

- *Yelp.* If your neighborhood is part of a larger community that has a downtown area, then take a few hours and review every business you like and use. Since your whole ethos is to be a positive promoter of the community, you should only write good reviews: if you can't say anything nice, say nothing. Then, take all those reviews and collect them into a "list" on Yelp and give it that SEO-friendly name. You'll be amazed at what happens. I collected all my Nyack restaurant reviews, created a list, titled it "Best Nyack Restaurants—From Joe Rand," and now when you Google the phrase "Best Nyack Restaurants," my list (and my name) often shows up in on the first page of organic results.

- *Website.* Finally, think about creating a website dedicated to the community. You don't need anything crazy: just get a decent domain and create a static site that's a placeholder for some pictures, SEO-friendly copy, and links to your other more dynamic online resources, including your business profiles. If you want to be more aggressive, get a developer to build you an IDX compliant inventory website, and maybe set it to execute an automatic search restricted to your local neighborhood every time someone visits. Even better, add an Automated Value Model to the site with a big "How Much is Your Home Worth?" link on the front page.

The best part of these online resources is that you can very cheaply and efficiently foster the impression that you are the foremost expert on that local area. Let's say, for example, you're at an open house in the area, meet a prospective buyer, and find out they don't know the neighborhood that well. What are they going to think when you show them your Facebook group, Pinterest board, Yelp lists, and community website? Why would they keep looking for an agent for that neighborhood?

But here's the catch: you still have to send direct mail. All these online assets are basically the air cover for your ground war. They're not a substitute. So you need to send out all the conventional mailings: Just Listed cards every time you take a listing, Just Sold cards every time you're involved in a sale, and so on. I would urge you, though, to mix in mailings that provide those Courtesy Services that homeowners need: information about the market, advice on property management, community guides, things like that. You're not just marketing yourself, you're providing a service to the community. That's the (metaphorical!) bottle of wine that you're bringing to the party.

Unrepresented Sellers

Willie Sutton is one of the most successful bank robbers in history, stealing an estimated $2 million in dozens of heists over his long career. Alas, he was also pretty good at getting caught, which led to several lengthy prison terms (and a few breakouts, because he was pretty good at that, too). But Willie Sutton is most famous for an apocryphal story about why he continued to rob banks, even after getting caught so many times. After all, banks had vaults, and alarms, and armed guards protecting them. Why take the risk?

His answer: "because that's where the money is."

It's the same thing with FSBO and Expired sellers: that's where the listings are.

Think of it this way: most of our lead generation techniques are designed to filter through the teeming masses of humanity to find the few people who are actually in the market. And yet, every day, you can just go online to find homeowners who are already selling their home and don't have a broker (i.e., FSBOs). And every day, the MLS spits out a list of people who are also selling their home and no longer have a broker (i.e., Expireds).

Think about that. All that work we do to find people who might be selling, and here we have big groups of homeowners who are already selling and need an agent.

So this should be easy, right? Well, according to traditional prospecting gurus, it is easy. Just make those calls! Call that FSBO and ask how long until he hires a professional to handle his sale. Call that Expired seller and taunt her with how many homes you've sold since she unsuccessfully went on the market.

That's why marketing to unrepresented sellers is so tough: because that well gets polluted pretty quickly. The opportunities are easily teed up, and the barriers to entry are virtually non-existent. You have to work long and hard to build a Sphere and a Top 100, good listing marketing requires expertise, open houses take time, and farms take money—but any fool agent with a phone and some hackneyed script book can call up and harangue some unrepresented FSBO and Expired sellers. So those sellers get a lot of solicitations, which hardens them to even the most well-meaning agent.

We should do better than this. We can do better than this. We just need to stop thinking of ourselves, and start thinking about our potential clients. What do they need, and how can we give it to them?

So what do these unrepresented sellers need?

FSBOs. Think about why someone sells his house on his own. It's to save money. That's it. Frankly, he would love it if we'd help him sell his house, he just doesn't want to pay us. He thinks that he can do what we do, and that in the end he can save money. And that's the key to understanding what he needs. He doesn't need someone to harangue him about when he'll give up and hire an agent. He needs someone to help him sell his home—for free!

So let's do that! Seriously, why not? I know it sounds crazy, but if we want to cultivate a relationship with that seller, in the hopes that when he's not successful selling on his own that he'll turn to us, we should try satisfying his need for some free help.

Now, calm down, I'm not talking about taking a listing for nothing. You're not going to do what you do for your actual sellers. You're not going to take pictures, or write marketing copy, or advise on staging, or do all of your listing marketing, or all that. No, you're just going to provide that seller with a Courtesy Service, like the free notarization at the lawyer's office, or using the lobby bathroom at the hotel. You're going to offer services that don't cost you anything, or take much time, but which create small amounts of goodwill that can build a relationship.

Here's the key: you're going to give him some help, but not the kinds of services that actually sell homes. You're going to provide some services that are helpful, and convenient, and thoughtful, but don't actually move the needle on getting that home sold. He doesn't deserve that kind of help unless he actually hires you. But, by being the kind of agent who respects him, who doesn't try to harangue him into listing, you create the kind of goodwill that will get you the opportunity to list it when he, like most FSBO sellers, fails.

So what are the services we provide a FSBO seller? At my company, we created something we called the "FSBO Courtesy Package," which contains a standardized set of materials:

- *Cover Letter.* A letter explaining that we respected the seller's decision to sell on his own but wanted to offer our help as a "courtesy."

- *Simple CMA.* A short CMA that didn't recommend a price but gave him an idea of activity in the market.

- *Market Report.* An analysis of real estate activity.

- *Vendor List.* A list for professionals he might need during his sale.

- *Showing Checklist.* A simple checklist of that long list of things that you need to do to get the home prepared for showings or open houses.

- *Sign-in Sheets.* A simple blank sign-in sheet for open houses or showings.

- *Promotional Material.* And some basic promotional material about the company, as a throw-in.

You see what I mean? None of those things are actually going to help him sell his house. Agents sometimes object that the CMA might help him price his home to the market, but any enterprising homeowner in your area has access to all the information he needs to do his own pricing: active listings, automated valuations, even sometimes sold data. This isn't 30 years ago, you're not the gatekeeper of that information. Even more than that, you know how hard it is to get sellers to price a home accurately, even with a full CMA, and even with you in the room to guide them! If that FSBO seller gets your Simple CMA and actually nails the pricing all on his own, more power to him.

But even though these services won't help sell the home, they're useful, the kind of thing that a professional might provide as a simple courtesy. Recommending a contractor or providing sign-in sheets isn't going to sell that house, but it's a thoughtful gesture.

Even more than that, though, you want the Courtesy Package to convey a subtle, almost subliminal, message: I'm not worried about you selling on your own, because selling a home is hard work. That's why I'm giving you all this as a courtesy.

Of course, like any mailing piece, the FSBO Courtesy Package is just a reason to call. So the day after you drop off the package, follow up with a phone call:

Hi, this is Joe Rand from Rand Realty, and I just wanted to call as a courtesy to wish you luck in your home sale. Also, I dropped off a Courtesy Package at your door yesterday, I wanted to see if you got it. Great! Please feel free to reach out if you have any questions, or I can be of any assistance.

Now, does any of this mean that you're going to get the listing? No, of course not. The seller might actually be successful on his own. Or he might get the right prospecting call at the right time, and just cave in. But you've certainly improved your chances of getting an appointment when the seller decides it's time to hire an agent. And all it took was a few minutes of your time and a little courtesy.

Expireds. The challenge with Expired sellers is a little different. If FSBOs are confirmed bachelors who never want to settle down,

Expireds are recent divorcees. They bought into the system—they got the ring, they walked down the aisle—and now that it didn't work out, they feel burned.

But the approach is basically the same: think expansively about what they need, and creatively about how to give it to them. What does the Expired seller need? Well, think about it from her perspective. She listed the home, went through all the trouble to get it ready, dealt with the showings, maybe got some offers, maybe even had a deal that fell through, all of that. Now, it's months later, and she has to start all over—and the very last thing she needs is a horde of agents taunting her about how many homes they sold over the past six months.

So what she needs is simple: she needs to know why her home didn't sell. What happened? Was it the price, marketing, condition, availability, what? She also wants reassurance that she's not a lost cause, that the home can still sell. Even more, she wants to know that it's not her fault.

And how are we going to service that need? By using the same system we used with FSBO sellers: create a standardized Courtesy Package customized only with a Simple CMA, drop it off. Indeed, many of the materials you can include are the same: cover letter, Simple CMA, market stats, and promotional materials.

The rest of the Expired Courtesy Package is designed to guide her through the process of understanding why her home didn't sell. And that's the key: you're not going to tell her, you're just going to give her the materials she needs to figure it out for herself. At my company, we developed an "Explainer," a short discussion about the three main reasons listings expire: condition, marketing, and price. Even better, the Explainer was attached to a "Self-Diagnostic" that gave the seller the opportunity to evaluate her listing by answering a series of yes/no questions about the staging, marketing, pricing, availability, etc. Indeed, the diagnostic was designed to set a vastly higher standard of best practices than most agents meet. So a seller going through the diagnostic was likely to find a lot of "Nos," areas where the prior agent didn't perform up to those standards.

But the key point is that the seller discovered this for herself. Too many times in expired listing campaigns, agents run really close to the line of making unethically critical comments on a colleague.

That's why we didn't put anything in the diagnostic that was inherently critical of the other agent. It was just a list of questions identifying best practices. If the former agent did a good job on that listing, and it expired despite his best efforts, then he would come out looking great. And if he didn't, then it wasn't us criticizing the agent, it was the seller coming to that judgment on her own. It's an objective performance evaluation, nothing more.

Indeed, the high standards also applied to us! That's one of the reasons I loved the self-diagnostic, because it required my own agents to adhere to those best practices. After all, they couldn't go ahead and send it to sellers if they didn't do great work staging, marketing, and pricing their own listings.

In other words, if they wanted to follow this system, they had to be great at their jobs.

Part One Conclusion: Be Great at Your Job

N̶o̶ ̶o̶n̶e̶ wants to be a "lead."

No one wants to be in your "farm."

No one deserves to be called a "FSBO," or an "Expired."

Our traditional prospecting methodology is all about what people can do for us, not what we can do for them. Even the terminology we use is reductive and dehumanizing, robbing our potential clients of their individuality and their agency. We talk about our "Spheres of Influence," as if our friends, family, and past clients revolve around us as the center of their universe, pulled by the gravitational force of our mesmerizing hypnotic powers. We talk about our "farms," as if homeowners are mindless vegetables. We define people solely by reference to our prospecting methodology—this person is a "FSBO," that one is an "Expired"—as if that status defines who they are.

Think about where the very concept of "prospecting" comes from: the old gold miners in Northern California sifting through mud and muck trying to find a nugget of gold. That's what we've been traditionally trained to do to people: treat them like mud and muck in our endless search for a rock we can polish up and make money from: a "lead."

It's all about us, not them.

Let's make it about them, and the services we can provide to them. Traditional prospecting taught us to think about our own needs and to treat potential clients like marks in a con-game. Modern Service-Oriented Lead Development (SOLD) treats lead generation as an opportunity to build relationships with people that will increase your chances of winning their business.

Indeed, the fundamental sources of business in SOLD are the same as traditional prospecting: build a Sphere, cultivate referrals, make calls, do open houses, farm, contact FSBOs and Expireds. The difference is the approach, the mindset. Rather than showing up at every interaction with nothing but a knife and a fork, you show up with a bottle of wine.

And, as always, if you're great at your job, all sorts of good things will happen for you:

If you're great at the job of providing the Sphere Courtesy Services to your Sphere, and positioning yourself as their real estate agent, you increase the chances that when they do need an agent to help them buy or sell a home, they'll turn to you.

If you're great at the job of providing those services to your Top 100 and adding in all the personalized touches that build that relationship, then you'll cultivate a group of people who will be evangelical in supporting your business with a steady, consistent stream of referrals.

If you're great at the job of listing marketing, then you'll sell more listings, and attract more buyers drawn in by your engaging work.

If you're great at the job of leveraging up your open houses with pre-marketing and post-follow-up, you'll get more visitors, which is good for both your seller and you.

If you're great at providing hyper-local informational services to your farm, you'll position yourself as the go-to agent for that neighborhood.

And if you're great at providing Courtesy Services to unrepresented sellers (FSBOs and Expireds), you'll increase your chances of getting an appointment to list or relist that home.

So be great.

Service-Oriented Lead Development Tools

Tool	Need	Service	Execution
Sphere	General real estate and community information.	Three Sphere Courtesy Services: market information, property management advice, and community updates.	Digital Service-and-Marketing program providing the Courtesy Services.
Top 100	General real estate and community information, plus personal attention.	Three Sphere Courtesy Services.	Digital and print Service-and-Marketing program providing the Courtesy Services, plus personal attention and phone calls/texts.
Just Listed Courtesy Calls	Need to know what's happening in the local neighborhood.	Alert neighbors to the possible disruption of your new listing.	Courtesy Call to block or neighborhood.
Listing Marketing	Seller needs marketing to help sell the home, and buyer needs information about homes for sale.	Market the home with engaging content to service both seller and buyer needs.	Beautiful marketing and follow up on all inquiries to answer their questions.
Open Houses	Sellers need to provide showings to early-stage buyers, and buyers need a way to see the home without an appointment.	Create a window for low-commitment showings, particularly by unrepresented buyers.	Leverage an event-open house with Courtesy Calls and listing marketing, and then follow up.
Community Development (i.e., Farming)	Need for neighborhood-based real estate and community information	The Sphere Courtesy Services tailored to a hyper-local market.	Mailings coupled with online "air support."
FSBO Marketing	Needs help and advice for selling his home.	The FSBO Courtesy Services: CMA, general advice and support.	A FSBO Courtesy Package, followed up by a Courtesy Call.
Expired Marketing	Needs to know why the home didn't sell, and reassurance that it can sell.	The Expired Courtesy Services: overview of why homes don't sell, self-diagnostic, and a CMA.	An Expired Courtesy Package followed up by a Courtesy Call.

Part Two:
Client Conversion

Talk less, listen more.

Chapter 5

The Consultative Presentation

MORE MONEY, MORE PROBLEMS.

A few years ago, once I started to make some decent money in real estate, I decided that I needed to hire a financial planner. I had never needed one before, because, you know, I was a teacher, and therefore didn't have any money that needed managing.

So I asked around, because when you're hiring someone for a job that requires a high degree of skill, you get personal referrals from friends. My brother recommended a planner named Jim, so my wife and I went to meet with him in his office. Our plan was to hear him out and see what we thought, but we didn't think we'd hire someone that day. We had a bunch of meetings with other planners set up.

We sat down, and everyone introduced themselves. Then Jim started asking us questions. Not in a "third degree" kind of way, but like someone who was interested in finding out about us. He asked about our personal and educational background, our living situation, how long we'd been married, our careers, things like that.

Then, eventually, he started moving into financial issues. How much money did we make? How much had we saved? How well did we understand the planning process? What kind of investments had we made in the past? What were our thoughts about the equities markets? About life insurance? About international investments? About fixed-income instruments? All that stuff.

And then he went even deeper, asking us some personal questions about our financial and personal goals. Did we plan on having kids? How many? When did we want to retire? What did we want to do after we retired?

It was almost an unsettling experience, because I found myself sharing things that I had never talked about before—even with my wife! And I was learning things about her that I'd never known, about her fears about money and hopes for retirement. The conversation became strikingly personal in less than an hour, as we both started to confide some of our most intimate thoughts about our future to Jim (and each other!).

That was a little weird, right? I mean, we had just met him less than an hour ago. We knew nothing about him. But here we were, confiding our innermost goals, dreams, and fears to him, telling him things we'd never even told each other in over 10 years together.

And a funny thing started to happen: I started to trust him. I even started to like him. It was almost a form of cognitive dissonance: if I didn't trust him, and I didn't like him, then what the heck was I doing telling him all this private stuff about me? If I'm confiding in him like this, then I must trust him, right? So I started to build faith in him, and so did my wife.

And it was a reinforcing dynamic: the more I trusted him, the more I confided, and the more I confided, the more I trusted him.

Now, here's the best part. This went on for over an hour, and during that entire time I don't think he ever told us anything about himself, his firm, his services, or his track record. He never talked about any of that. He just asked us questions about ourselves and listened to what we had to say.

Eventually, of course, he did turn the conversation to what he could do for us. Now that he knew our familiarity with planning, our tolerance for risk, and our financial goals, he explained the services he provided and showed us how those services connected to the needs we'd already expressed. Even then, though, he didn't talk much about himself. He just talked about what he did, and how it would help us.

At the end of the conversation, we didn't even have to make a decision about hiring him to manage our money. We'd already made that decision during the course of that conversation, when we opened up to him. We agreed right there to hire him, and later canceled all the other appointments.

And as I left his office, happy with our decision, feeling good about my future, a thought occurred to me:

Why don't real estate agents do that?

I mean, that financial planning meeting was basically what we would think of as a "listing presentation." I needed to hire someone to help me through a challenging financial process, and was interviewing a candidate for the job. But the dynamic between my meeting with Jim and the conventional listing presentation could not have been more different.

For one thing, the traditional listing presentation is completely agent-oriented. We teach agents to talk about themselves: their track record, their awards, their reviews, their testimonials, their company, their 27-point marketing program, and so on. It's all about them. We even train agents that when they're reviewing pricing with a seller, they should forcefully remind the seller that they are the "experts," and that the seller should "trust them" on price. Why? Because it's all about the agent.

Even worse, the traditional listing presentation is taught as if it's a performance, almost like the agent is putting on some sort of show. Indeed, even the way we talk about listing presentations uses terms more appropriate for the theater. We encourage agents to "rehearse" their presentation with their manager or coach and give them "scripts" to memorize and recite at the right time: "this way, I can get you what you want in the time you want—won't that be great?!" The presentation is basically an "audition" for the role of "real estate agent."

We've been doing it all wrong. The traditional listing presentation is a terrible way to meet with a client, completely counter-productive to the relationship we're trying to establish. The sales-y approach puts the client on guard, skeptical and suspicious of our motivations. Moreover, the traditional presentation is a lot of work! It's really hard memorizing all those scripts, and it's stressful trying to perform like that under pressure.

And we're even worse with buyers! Buyers don't even get that well-rehearsed listing presentation. Sellers get hours of prep, slick materials, a whole song-and-dance routine. It's terrible, but at least we're trying. With buyers, we just meet them at the house they called on. If we do bring them in before-hand, we spend five minutes with them. No prep. No slick materials. No song. No dance.

We don't need to do it this way. Look at how Jim ran his interview with my wife and me. The meeting wasn't about him, it was about us. He spent 90% of his time asking us questions about ourselves, not talking about himself, his track record, his company, his services, his awards, or any of it. His emphasis was on finding out about us: our needs, our fears, our goals. And it wasn't any kind of "performance." He wasn't putting on some sort of show, he was engaging us in a conversation, and it's certainly a lot easier to ask a lot of prepared questions than it is to execute on a script. Finally, we never felt like he was trying to "sell" us anything. He was, of course. He was persuading us to hire him to manage our money. But the feel of the meeting was more like a consultation in a doctor's or lawyer's office than a pitch at a retail store.

And that's the key word right there: consultation. Service professionals like doctors, lawyers, and financial planners don't do "presentations," they perform "consultations." They meet you with the purpose of identifying what your problem is, and how they can solve it. And it's not just white-collar professionals: the same goes for service providers like plumbers or electricians. Think about the last time you brought in someone to work on your home. Did they come in and spend an hour telling you about their credentials, and trying to pitch you on hiring them? They don't talk about themselves, they don't put on a show, and they don't try to sell you. They find out what's wrong, and they tell you how they can fix it. Their expertise sells itself.

The whole mindset is different. They're not meeting with you to audition for the job. They're meeting with you because that's the first step toward solving your problem.

Even better: the meeting itself is part of that service. Indeed, it's the first service they provide, the very act of finding out what you need from them.

That's what we need to do. Stop thinking of the initial meeting as a presentation, and start thinking about it as a consultation—as the first of the many services we're going to provide that client.

That's what CORE is all about. The CORE Formula starts with thinking expansively about what people need. Consider some of the things they might need at that initial listing meeting with you:

- an overview of the process of selling their home;

- an analysis of the pricing environment in their market, and help in setting the initial price for their home;

- an explanation of the services the agent will be providing;

- guidance on preparing their home for sale (i.e., staging);

- reassurance that their home will sell; and

- someone who will patiently explain all of this, and answer all of their questions about the process.

But you can't do any of that if you go in with some rote script that you memorized and rehearsed with your manager. Every client is different, and every client needs different things from you at that initial consultation. You don't know what they need, though, until you start asking the questions and gauging their responses.

We have to stop giving conventional one-size-fits-all performances with 100-year old scripts. We have to stop trying to manipulate people into hiring us. And we have to stop talking about ourselves, and start focusing on our clients.

So in this part, we're going to talk about the consultative presentation, and how a client-oriented approach can dramatically change the dynamic of the traditional presentation. Specifically, we're going to talk mostly about the listing presentation with sellers, but we'll finish this part with a review of best practices for buyer presentations as well.

Of course, a great listing consultation starts not when you walk in the door, but in your preparation. Here's what you need to do in advance:

1. *Confirmation Call.* Make a confirmation call to the client to confirm the appointment and gather some useful information to help you prepare your CMA. Also, you use that call to ensure that all the decision-makers will be there, and to ask the sellers to take some steps (pull documents together,

get a set of keys) that gets them used to listening to you and following your instructions.

2. *Research.* Research the property by gathering all the information you can on your MLS, RPR, or any other resource, and also research the sellers on Google and social media to find out all you can about them.

3. *Orientation Package.* You should drop off or send an "Orientation Package" to the seller, consisting of all the materials you'd like them to review prior to your meeting: samples of your marketing, testimonials, references, explainers, and marketing pieces. The purpose of the package is to persuasively introduce yourself and explain the process of selling a home. Moreover, it's a good way to give the sellers all the materials they need to read, so that they're not reading while you're trying to talk with them.

4. *CMA.* You prepare your CMA and even start looking over and printing the Automated Value Models (AVMs) you want to use in your Pricing Analysis.

5. *Showpieces.* Pull together your "Showpieces," which are the illustrations for your marketing and service presentation, things like your direct mail pieces, market-share reports, and anything else that will vividly support your points without needing to be read.

You do all that in advance, then get to the appointment five minutes early so you can prepare yourself in the car. Pull all your things together, go to the door, smile, and knock. Introduce yourself. Give the clients a small gift to thank them for having you in the home (just like my grandmothers taught me!). Take a tour of the home, saying nice things and writing notes for later. Then sit down in the kitchen or living room, pull everything out, and get started with the consultation:

- First, you'll start with what we'll call the "Needs Consultation," where you build rapport with your clients by asking the questions about them, their concerns about the selling process, and their expectations for you as their agent.

- Second, you're going to present what we'll call the "Project Plan"—a presentation about all the work you're going to provide to help your clients through the selling process and get their home sold. The key to the "Project Plan" is separating out the various services you provide, illustrating them through the Showpieces, and differentiating yourself from your competitors.

- Third, once you're done explaining the Project Plan, you're actually going to start providing the most important service an agent gives a client: the Pricing Analysis. But instead of using that CMA to tell the seller what the price should be, you're going to frame your Pricing Analysis as one of the first crucial services you're going to provide that seller, educating the sellers about the pricing process and collaborating with them on setting the initial price for the home.

That's the CORE consultative listing presentation: Needs Consultation, Project Plan, Market Analysis.

The key to the CORE consultative approach is that this initial meeting is not a "pitch." You're not there trying to convince a prospect to list her home with you. Instead, that initial meeting is the first vital service you provide your new clients: consulting with them about their concerns, educating them about the process, and learning what you need to do to give them a great experience throughout the entire transaction. Indeed, as you'll see, you can actually provide three CORE services at that initial meeting, because you'll not only be consulting with them, but you'll be guiding them through the process of pricing their home, and, once the documents are signed, advising them on what they need to do to detail and stage the home for maximum impact on buyers.

But that all comes later. To start, you're simply going to ask questions, and listen.

Chapter 6

The Needs Consultation: It's Not About You

I WAS ON VACATION IN MEXICO, I'D SPENT THE ENTIRE day at the beach, and I was exhausted. Yeah, I know, woe is me, right? But anytime you spend the day in the sun, you're going to be a little wiped out.

So I was in no mood to go out to dinner with a bunch of couples my wife and I had met at the resort. They seemed like nice people and all, but I was just too tired to talk to anyone. Even worse, we all sat in a jumble, and I was on the opposite end of the table from my wife, so I couldn't even rely on her to carry me.

That's how I found myself sitting next to this nice woman, Erin, from Texas, who was there with a husband who was also sitting far away. We were stuck with each other, and we had to make conversation.

But I was in no mood to put in any real effort. In a lot of these situations, I feel the pressure to be funny or entertaining, it's sort of built into my DNA. But not tonight. I didn't want to "entertain" her or tell jokes or whatever. Honestly, I just wanted to take a nap with my head nestled warmly in the conch chowder.

So what did I do? I just started asking her questions about herself. I figured that would be easier: let her carry the conversation. She seemed interesting enough, so I could let her entertain me!

It turned out she was starting a business, so I was able to ask what I thought were pretty relevant questions about her plans, the industry, all that stuff. And it actually went pretty well. Dinner passed reasonably quickly. She was interesting, the business idea was intriguing, and we had a nice conversation. And she did all the work! I was just asking question after question. I'm not sure I made a declarative statement over the course of the entire two hours.

When dinner was over, we all went for some drinks and mingled. My wife, whom I hadn't spoken to for the entire dinner, came up to me, and we had this conversation:

"Hey, how was dinner?" I asked.

"It was fun," she said. "How about you? Looked like you were having a good conversation."

"Oh, really? Yeah, I guess. I was so tired, she did most of the talking."

At which point Erin came up to us, put her arm around my wife, and said:

"Oh, you are so lucky..."

Which is true!

"... Your husband is wonderful! ..."

Also true!

"... And so smart!"

Huh?

Now, I'm not denying any of this. I am indeed wonderful. And very smart! But why would she think that? I barely spoke, never ventured an opinion, didn't give any advice, or do anything that might have impressed her with my smarts.

It didn't matter.

Why did she like me? Because I showed an authentic interest in her.

And why did she think I was smart? Because I listened to what she had to say.

Most people never get it. Single guys go out, and think they'll impress their dates by talking all about themselves, flashing a peacock's tail to show how interesting they are. Real estate agents meet a client, and think they'll convince that client to work with them by talking about themselves, showing how impressive their credentials are.

That's not how it works. You don't connect with people by talking about yourself, you connect by showing an interest in them, and letting them talk about themselves. We are all our favorite subject. That's not narcissism, it's just basic human nature. We all think we're interesting, and we're all flattered and intrigued when someone else seems to agree.

So whether you're a single guy on a date or a real estate agent on a listing appointment, the lesson is the same: talk less, listen more.

The Needs Consultation

Remember that the foundation of CORE is simple: focus on what other people need, not your own needs. It's about them, not you.

Indeed, the best way to build a real rapport with someone is to show an authentic interest in them. That's true whether you're on a first date, sitting with someone at a dinner party, or at a listing presentation. That's why you want to start every listing appointment with the "Needs Consultation," where you ask a series of questions to your sellers designed to get to know them better.

Here are exactly seven reasons why:

1. *It establishes the right mindset for you.* The classic listing presentation is an agent-centric production right from the beginning, with the agent usually launching into a recitation of her background, her company, her awards, and all that. And that sets the tone for the rest of the presentation, which focuses on the agent's marketing plan and puts the agent at the center of the pricing discussion as the "expert you should trust."

But we're going to flip that mindset in the CORE approach: from agent-oriented to client-oriented. Starting with the Needs Consultation shows that you value that client's uniqueness—that you're rejecting the "one-size-fits-all" mentality that characterizes the traditional listing presentation. Since every client is different, your first responsibility as an agent is to find out how this client is different.

So instead of talking about yourself, you're going to ask questions to find out more about the clients. That helps affix the right mindset for your appointment: it's not about you, it's about them.

2. *It establishes the right mindset for your client.* Starting with the Needs Consultation also establishes the mindset you want for your client: you are not there on some sort of "audition," you are there to begin servicing their needs and solving their problem. Your presentation should evoke the experience of visiting a doctor or lawyer, someone who takes the time to find out what the problem is before

trying to solve it, and who doesn't feel the compulsion to convince you to hire her.

Think about how that changes the whole dynamic of your presentation. You're not there to convince the seller to hire you. You've already been hired! And since you've already been hired, your job now is to get to know the clients better and show them how you're going to take great care of them.

Ultimately, this creates the mindset that you want for the rest of the presentation. You don't want the clients feeling like they're meeting with someone trying to sell them some manufacturer-direct custom blinds.

3. You'll build rapport. I can't tell you how many terrible conference sessions I've seen where a trainer promises he can teach you how to build rapport with a client through some sort of hoary manipulative technique: "As you walk through the home, take note of what you see and use that to find common ground. If the seller has a lot of pictures of sailboats, tell her that you like sailing, too! Is she a Yankees fan? Well, so are you!"—Horrible stuff.

You also get trainers promising to teach agents how to build rapport through tricks like "neurolinguistic programming" ("NLP"), in which you mimic a client's gestures and speech patterns to form a subconscious bond. It's silly. For one thing, NLP is really, really hard, and not something you can learn in a 90-minute conference session or even a full-day training event. More importantly, if you're not really good at NLP, then your attempts to "mirror" your client will come across like some sort of robotic affectation. You won't build rapport, you'll just look like an idiot. Put it this way: if you have the capacity to master NLP, go to work in an industry with bigger margins where you can make more money than real estate.

Even worse, NLP is unnecessary. Ultimately, the best way to establish rapport is just to be authentically interested in what the other person has to say. Ask questions, listen to the answers, take notes, show an interest in what they're saying, and engage them in a conversation about their needs. More importantly, be yourself. Don't try to fake who you are. You'll almost certainly never pull it off, and rather than build rapport you'll come across as insincere and inauthentic.

4. You'll earn trust. The more people confide in you, the more they trust you. Think of it this way. If I start telling you private things about myself, things I don't normally talk about with other people, then I'm going to feel a lot of internal pressure to trust you. Why? Because, if I didn't trust you, then why in the world am I telling you all those private things about myself? In other words, the very act of confiding in someone builds trust with that person, almost by default.

This is exactly what happened in my own financial planning consultation with Jim. He got me talking about myself to the point that I had no choice but to trust him. He didn't manipulate or trick me, he just got me talking about myself, and I did the rest.

You can do the same thing. If you can get your clients to open up to you about their concerns about the selling process, their fears about their home not selling, their hopes for the future, and any other private issues, then they're going to feel that internal drive to trust you.

5. You'll generate commitment from your clients. The more people confide in you, the more they trust you, the more they like you, then the more they're going to feel committed to working with you. A great consultation opens up the client in such a personal way that the client will start thinking of you as "their agent" before you've even told them about any of your services. Indeed, they might develop such a bond with you that they'd consider it "disloyal" to even meet with any other agents!

Think of your own history with service professionals. After meeting with your doctor, how many times did you actually go get a "second opinion" from another? How often have you gone to more than one lawyer for a consultation? Or met with two or three electricians? Yes, of course, sometimes we do bid a project out, but most of the time when we've found someone we like and trust, we don't shop around. We make a commitment.

That's the kind of dynamic you want in your presentation. Your very mindset should prompt you to speak assumptively and collaboratively (i.e., "when we market our listing," not "if I market your listing"), in a way that will support your clients' commitment to working with you.

6. You'll gather information for the rest of the presentation. We've talked a lot about how starting with the Needs Consultation establishes the right interpersonal dynamic for the rest of your presentation, but you also get a very practical benefit: you gather a lot of helpful information! After all, you're asking a lot of questions, and you're bound to learn something from your clients that will help tailor the rest of your presentation.

You might discover, for example, that they once had a bad experience with a real estate agent who completely lost touch with them, which allows you to focus your Project Plan on your commitment to ongoing client communication. Or you might find that they're really concerned about a foreclosure down the block that might impact their pricing, so you can emphasize how you would handle that in your Pricing Analysis. These are all issues that you would never uncover if you launched right into your canned spiel about your 27-point marketing plan.

The key, of course, is not just to ask questions. You need to listen to the answers, take notes, and adapt the rest of your presentation to what you learn.

7. *It's easier!* Finally, because the CORE approach to the presentation is to focus on the client, not on you, the pressure is off. The Needs Consultation is a lot easier than launching into a traditional listing presentation. You don't have to deliver a series of memorized scripts. You don't have to put on a show. You don't even have to carry the conversation. Instead, you can be like me at that beach dinner: asking questions, listening to answers, and allowing the conversation to develop naturally.

Now, you might have parts of your presentation that you'll want to have prepared, particularly when you talk about your services and marketing, or when you explain the pricing process. But the Needs Consultation gives you a chance to get warmed up to that, to settle in a little.

The bottom line: it's a lot harder to answer questions than to ask them. So why not make things a little easier on yourself?

The Needs Consultation Methodology

Okay, so now that you know why you're going to start with the Needs Consultation, let's talk about how you're going to do it.

First, always sit next to your clients, not across from them. Throughout your presentation, you need to maintain a soothing physical posture, one that relaxes rather than alarms your clients. One way to do this is to make sure that you never sit across from your clients—that is, don't sit down at a table with them on one side and you on the other. Rather, try to sit at a corner of a table or couch that puts you at an angle to your clients, which creates a more casual, collegial, and collaborative environment. Studies show that sitting across from someone can seem confrontational, and make someone feel defensive, like you're gunslingers facing off in the Old West. You certainly do not want to evoke that kind of reaction. You're not there to negotiate with them, you're there to work with them. So try sitting to the side, so you're not going at them face-to-face.

Second, listen actively. You're trying to have a conversation, not an inquisition. This isn't the "third degree." Don't just rattle off a bunch of disconnected questions. You need to pay attention to what they're telling you and respond with conversational "connectors" that will show your engagement: follow up with "how," "when," and "why" questions to dig deeper, use non-verbal gestures like nodding your head to keep them talking, and repeat their statements as questions to get them to elaborate. And have a pad of paper ready to take notes, which not only shows that you're paying attention but also acts as a signifier of a professional consultation—the way that doctors and lawyers meet with patients and clients.

Third, use collaborative language to generate a sense of commitment. Use "when" phrases rather than "if" phrases: "when (not if) we get the home on the market," "when (not if) we get offers," "when (not if) we get the home sold"—language that presumes that you will be taking that listing. Why? Because every time you make that presumption, and the client doesn't stop you, you firm up the connection you're making between agent and client. You want them to start getting used to the idea of you as their agent, which will help you build trust. And use language that makes you all part of the same team: "we" instead of "you." Whenever possible, talk about how "we" are going to get the home on the market, and how "our" listing is going to look. You want to foster the feeling that you're in this together, and you've already started the process of representing them.

Finally, prepare an exhaustive list of questions that you can ask during the consultation. At my company, we have a "Consultation Guide" that provides dozens of potential questions along with spaces where you can take notes, but it's mostly designed as a crutch for agents just so they don't freeze up when they sit down with their clients.

You should do the same thing: prepare a list of standard questions that you want to ask your clients, and print it with adequate room for you to take notes during the consultation.

Here are some of the issues you want to make sure you ask about, and why you might find them important throughout your presentation:

- *Motivation.* Ask about their personal situation: why they are moving, where they are going, and how quickly do they need to move?

- *Process.* Probe their understanding of the home-selling process and identify any concerns they might have.

- *Positives.* Ask their opinion on what they think is the strongest selling feature of the home, or who the likely buyer will be. Asking the seller's opinion about the home they've lived in for years shows respect for them and gets them engaged in the process. Moreover, the "little things" that people only learn about a home once they've lived in it can sometimes be really effective in preparing your marketing.

- *Challenges.* Conversely, you also want your clients to help you identify the challenges you're likely to face in selling the home. What do they see as the biggest drawbacks of living in the home? What do they think will be the biggest objections potential buyers will have to making an offer? Again, sometimes homeowners are the best resources for this kind of information, which can be really helpful in tuning your marketing or showing strategies. Also, you might find it helpful to focus your seller's attention on some of the problems with the home, so that they go into the pricing discussion with open eyes.

- *Mechanics.* Confirm some of the mechanics of showing and marketing the home. When can the home be available for showings? Do the sellers have pets? Do they have any valuables they're concerned about? Do they have any privacy concerns about photos and videos? Just asking these questions can have an assumptive effect, that you're already working on how you're going to show and market the property.

- *Details*. Make sure you establish all the property details. Confirm the number of bedrooms, bathrooms, and other features. Find out whether they've done any work on the home, and whether they've got current certificates of occupancy.

- *Communication*. Find out how they want you to communicate with them. Do they want you to reach out to both of them, or is one person taking the lead? Do they want you to visit personally, call, text, email, or what? Establishing their preferences is crucial for ensuring a good relationship during the listing process.

- *Expectations*. Finally, you absolutely have to establish what they expect from an agent. You need to ask questions about their past experiences with agents and other service professionals, so you can get a sense of what they like and don't like. And you need to specifically ask what they expect of you, so you can adjust the rest of your presentation accordingly.

The key point to remember when you're going through your Needs Consultation is that you want to spark a conversation. Ideally, you won't even need to look at your list of questions, because the dialogue will naturally flow as you get to know your clients.

If you want to see a more exhaustive list of questions you can prepare for your Needs Consultation, check out the Agent Resource section of www.joerand.com.

Chapter 7

The Project Plan:
The CORE Services

HERE'S A TALE OF TWO PITCHERS.

Tom Seaver was one of the greatest pitchers in major league history, a first ballot hall-of-famer. Coming up with the New York Mets in the 1960s, he was a phenom, a power pitcher with a fastball that he could throw over 95 miles per hour. For a ten-year period with the Mets from 1967-1976, he struck out over 200 batters a season, blowing them away with his velocity.

As he got older, though, he started to lose some of his power (like, uh, many of us!). For the next ten years, he only averaged about 120 strikeouts per year, and only topped 200 one time. But he still won. Indeed, he recorded over 150 wins *after* his 30th birthday, even as his fastball gradually diminished.

Why was he still so effective? Because Seaver learned to pitch, not just throw. He couldn't rely on his fastball anymore, so he found new ways to get hitters out. He figured out how to change speeds, probe a batter's weak spots in the strike zone, create late movement, and even how to play to an umpire's individual tendencies. He adapted, and eventually won more than 300 games.

Our second pitcher is Kerry Wood, who is most decidedly *not* one of the greatest pitchers in major league history, even though he may have thrown the best game ever pitched. In 1998, at the age of 20, in only his fifth major league start, Wood struck out a record-setting 20 batters in nine innings. According to observers, he was throwing 95 mph fastballs that moved like wiffleballs. He didn't get the no-hitter, because he gave up a lucky infield single; nevertheless, many baseball historians call it the most dominating pitching performance ever seen.

But for all his natural talent and ability, Wood won't be getting named to the hall-of-fame. Early in his career, he suffered a series of injuries that robbed him of his incredible fastball. And, unlike Seaver, he never learned to pitch without that kind of dominating velocity. Toward the end of his relatively short career, he bounced around the league, finishing up as a reliever in the bullpen. His career total? Under 100 wins. A great thrower, but not a great pitcher.

Sadly, the real estate industry is like Kerry Wood—we haven't adapted to losing our fastball.

Here's what I mean: back before the internet era, clients needed real estate agents and brokers to get information about the real estate market, and to access the pool of buyers who were looking for a home. Why? Because we controlled access to the inventory, and access to the buyer pool.

We were the gatekeepers. If you wanted to sell a property, you had to list with an agent in order to offer the home through the multiple listing services to all the other agents and the buyers they represented. If you didn't, no one would even know your property was for sale, unless they stumbled across the sign or your small FSBO classified ad.

Similarly, if you wanted to buy a home, you had to go to one of those member agents to gain access to that MLS network and the inventory available. That's the only way you could even find out about the homes that were on the market.

That all changed, of course, when the internet opened that gate, giving anyone with a computer access to the real estate inventory that we'd controlled for so long. Sellers no longer needed to hire a broker to enter their home into the marketplace, especially once they could sell on their own and still list their property on most major real estate portals, and buyers no longer needed agents to see what homes were for sale, since they could just fire up the websites and see for themselves.

The gatekeeping role? That was our fastball. When we controlled access to the inventory, we didn't really have to do much else. Just throw the heater past them.

But when we lost the fastball, we didn't do enough to adapt. Too many agents are still relying on the same toolset and skillset that we used when we were gatekeepers. For example, they still make a big deal in their listing presentations about how they're going to market that listing on syndication portals like Zillow, Trulia, Realtor.com, Homes.com, Homesnap, and the rest. In other words, they're still stressing how their value comes from managing the exposure of the property—opening and closing the gate. But most MLS systems distribute listings across the internet free for all their members. A seller can list with pretty much any agent in your market and get the same syndication marketing that they get with you. Indeed, they don't even need to list with an agent; they can submit their listing to the portals on their own. We don't control access to the inventory anymore.

Similarly, we don't control access to the buyer pool, either. But we still try to act like we do. Too many listing presentations, for example, are built on the fiction that the broker or agent has exclusive connections to a unique buyer population: either "global high-end buyers" or "extensive relocation networks." The idea is that, if you list with that broker, you'll get special access to all those buyers. But is that really true? I get why franchise and referral networks can be good for agents, since they generate potential buyer leads. But why is any of that valuable for sellers? If that seller lists with you, does that give her any advantage in accessing that buyer population? Do you really control those buyers? Do you restrict the buyers' ability to find listings, or see listings, or buy listings? Of course not! Not when every one of those buyers can open an app on their phone and see everything that's available in your market.

In other words, our value to clients no longer comes from our gatekeeping role. We don't control access to information about the inventory, and we don't control access to buyers. We lost that fastball.

But that doesn't mean that real estate agents no longer provide value. We absolutely do. It's just that we can't simply rely on our role as gatekeepers of access to information about real estate. Rather, we have to find new ways to articulate the value we actually provide, in everything we do throughout the real estate transaction.

In other words, we need to learn how to pitch.

The Project Plan: The CORE Services

Before my wife became a real estate agent, she was a project manager with a major consulting firm, working with clients on massive technology implementations. Her job was to help the client set out a project, organize all the personnel, and then manage the process from beginning to end. The value she provided was in getting the job done, on time and on budget, while giving that client an excellent service experience.

Um... does that sound familiar?

So when she became an agent, she was amazed at how well her work in consulting had prepared her for working with real estate clients. It was the same job. Work with the client on setting out a plan. Organize all the moving parts. Manage the process. Provide value by getting the home sold, on the best possible terms, with a great client experience.

That's the way you should think about, and explain, your role to your clients: the project is the home sale, the Project Plan is your articulation of the services you're going to provide, and your job as the Project Manager is to manage that process from consultation to closing, coordinating all the other moving parts of the transaction to give them a great experience.

So what's the actual Project Plan? It's an articulation of all the work you're going to do for that seller. For example, in my book *Disruptors, Discounters, and Doubters,* I identified what I called the Seven CORE Services that agents provide to sellers:

1. *Counseling.* We find out about the sellers' specific needs by asking them questions, listening to their answers, and helping them understand and prepare for the process of selling a home.

2. *Pricing.* We help sellers understand the current market conditions and guide them through the process of pricing their home at the best possible price that will get that home sold.

3. *Staging.* We advise the sellers on the work they need to do to present the home more attractively to potential buyers.

4. *Marketing.* We create beautiful content and advertise the home to the largest possible audience while also targeting the most likely buyers.

5. *Negotiation.* We solicit all offers from buyers, present them to the sellers, and then advise on negotiating the best possible terms for the deal.

6. *Transaction Management.* We manage all our sellers' transactions from that accepted offer through the inspection, mortgage, title, walkthrough, and closing process.

7. *Communication.* And throughout the process, we communicate clearly and transparently, keeping them up-to-date on every development.

These are the core/CORE services: core because they are fundamental, and CORE because they're "Client-Oriented."

And here's the best part: they're actually real services. They're not misleading or meaningless. They're not antiquated remnants of our gatekeeping role. And if you're great at your job, that means you're going to do a better job of providing those services, so they're actually meaningful points of differentiation between you and your competitors. That's why our listing presentations need to explain the services we actually provide.

So let's go over each of the CORE Seller Services in a little more detail:

1. Counseling. At this point, you should have already differentiated yourself from most agents by going through the Needs Consultation. Most agents, as we know, will simply ignore the client and launch into their rehearsed presentation. So now that you're talking about your Project Plan, you explain how that Needs Consultation fits into the overall scheme:

You might have noticed that we've spent more of our time here talking about you. That's one of the most important services I provide: finding out about your particular needs. In my experience, every seller is different, so it's important to me that I find out what you really need from me, so that I can customize the rest of my services to you.

That's what the "Needs Consultation" is all about—it's the first major service we provide to our clients, and we do it before they even sign with us. So make clear that you're not in that meeting to sell your services; you're there to start finding out what the clients need, and advise them accordingly. And that's a really important service you provide, not just at the presentation, but throughout the process.

2. Pricing. We don't talk about pricing as a service. We provide it, usually right at the meeting, but we think of it as just another part of the listing presentation itself.

But pricing is one of the most important things that we do. Helping a seller identify the best possible price that will get the home sold, and guiding that seller away from overpricing the home, is maybe the most crucial service that we provide. Put it this way: if we do a good job helping the seller with the pricing, and flounder on everything else, we probably still stand a pretty good chance of getting that home sold. But if we fail, and the seller massively overprices the listing, then it doesn't matter how good we are at marketing and staging. That home is going to sit, and we're never going to get a chance to provide negotiating or transaction management services.

The biggest challenge, of course, is that being great at advising sellers on pricing often means convincing sellers to rein in their exuberant optimism about how much their home is worth. Great agents do that, which is why their listings sell. But it's not the best marketing pitch—"I'm great at my job because I keep you from doing something dumb like overpricing your listing." That's not what sellers want to hear. They want to hear how you're so great at your job that they can go ahead and overprice it!

That's why we need to frame our "pricing" service as a collaborative process that we guide clients through, not as a decision we make and then try to impose on them. The service is not telling them what the price should be, but guiding them to an understanding of the market. And the pricing service doesn't end at the listing presentation. It's just beginning, because you're going to advise them about how the market is reacting to your pricing strategy, and about how conditions are changing, throughout the entire time their home is on the market.

3. Staging. Let me ask you this question: what percentage of the homes for sale right now in your market are in beautiful showing condition? Half? Less than half?

In my experience, less than a third of homes for sale in most markets are in good showing condition. Why? Because most agents don't provide staging services to their clients. Somehow, we have gotten into our heads that staging is only for high-end luxury properties, and that it can only be done by "professional stagers." So we don't do it for most of our listings, and reserve it for upscale sellers that can afford to hire those outside consultants.

This may be the single biggest industry fail of the modern real estate era. We would never accept that we're not competent to price a home, and encourage the seller to bring in an appraiser. We would never accept that we're not capable of marketing a home, and delegate it out to an advertising agency. We're real estate agents. We provide pricing services. We provide marketing services. And we should provide staging services.

All real estate agents are already professional stagers; they just don't know it yet. This idea that we need outside consultants is nonsense. Most of staging is simple cleaning, decluttering, and depersonalizing. Are you telling me you need to be an interior decorator to figure out that the seller should clear out the cobwebs from the front stoop? That you need to go to design school to know that closets look better when they're half empty than bulging with clothes that the sellers will never wear again? Staging is not rocket science. You can learn it.

And your clients need it. We know the difference that staging can make, which makes it a dereliction of our fiduciary duty that we let them put their homes on the market in the condition that they're usually in. Yes, it's difficult to talk to sellers about why they can't sell their home like they've lived in it. But most of your clients are a lot more familiar with the concept of "staging" than you think. The myriad of makeover shows on cable television has almost made it a staple of home presentation, which means that you need to make it an arrow in your quiver. Indeed, I advise agents to talk about staging as "detailing," because most people have detailed their car in preparation for selling it, so they understand the concept and are less intimidated by it.

We still need professional staging consultants, of course, for the types of properties we usually refer to them now: truly unique high-end luxury homes that would benefit from a decorator's eye.

But most listings only need simple cleaning and de-cluttering, which means we are entirely capable of providing those services ourselves—to all our clients.

That's why you can really differentiate yourself in most markets by providing staging services directly for all your clients. Most agents don't do it because they (wrongly) think they're unqualified, and most discounters don't do it because staging is a labor-intensive responsibility that you can't provide at scale for a minimal commission—and you can't do it from a call center in India. So if you learn how to stage, and you make it part of your core (CORE!) value package, you can stand out in the market.

Indeed, staging is something—like pricing—that you can start doing right at the presentation. Take notes while you walk through the home on the recommendations you'd make, and, when you discuss your staging services, make it clear you have a lot of ideas for them that you'll share just as soon as you get through all the paperwork. Don't give that milk away for free!

4. Marketing. We need to talk about marketing differently. We're still stuck in the mindset that effective marketing involves distributing information about a listing to a broad audience. But free MLS syndication has basically commodified broad-based real estate marketing. Instead, we need to think of (and talk about) marketing as narrow, not broad. Focused, not diffused. In just the last few years, we've all gained access to an array of amazing data-based tools for targeting hyper-specific audiences, which we should be using to customize our marketing to the most probable buyers for our listings. Marketing today is not about distributing listings to a generalized audience, it's about using those tools to target our advertising narrowly to very specific types of consumers.

That should be your differentiator—not that you put the home on Zillow, which everyone does, and which is mostly a place for window-shoppers anyway. Rather, what you do is aggressively reach out to the types of people that are most likely to want this home. That's what makes you different.

Moreover, great marketing is now about beautiful content: gorgeous photos, engaging descriptions, clever videos, 3D walkthroughs, and impressive collateral. Create excellent content, and it not only helps sell that home, but it helps sell you when you lay it all out at your next listing consultation as evidence about how great you are at your job.

5. Negotiation. We all know that negotiation is a crucial service we provide our sellers, and yet we still don't really talk about it much at the listing presentation. We need to, because great negotiating skills make a difference for our clients.

Why don't we talk about it more? Part of it is that there's not much to talk about. Discussing marketing is easy, because you have all sorts of sexy stuff to pull out of your briefcase or tablet. And if you ever do talk about staging, you can always illustrate your ability through those "before and after" photos that everyone loves.

But how do you demonstrate your ability at negotiating? It's not easy, but here are some suggestions:

- Ask one of your favorite clients to write you a recommendation specifically about your negotiating ability, which you can wave around in your presentation.

- Try to find a metric that shows your negotiating performance. Like, do you sell your listings for closer to the asking price than the average agent? If so, you can make a graph out of that.

- Get some sort of third-party credential, like a certification or designation, specifically about your negotiation skills.

- Have a simple story to tell, something relatable that shows off your negotiating ability, like the time you negotiated a great deal that exceeded your clients' expectations.

Again, you're never going to generate the kind of illustrative flourish that you get for marketing and staging, but you want to have something visual and tangible for your presentation, if only to prompt you to actually talk about negotiation as an individualized service you provide.

6. Transaction Management. Selling a home is hard. We need to stop making it look easy.

That's what we do. We make it look easy. Why? Because we don't want to scare people. Because we treat clients like these timid little birds tentatively pecking at seeds in our outstretched hands, as if we're worried that the slightest provocation is going to scare them away.

So we hide the truth. We don't tell sellers how horrible it is to live in a home for sale, that they're going to have to deal with people traipsing in and out of their house at all hours of the day, making rude comments about their design taste. Even worse, we don't highlight how they're going to have to clean up after themselves until they get into contract. No more dishes in the sink!

In fact, I've often said that states should have a licensing requirement that all real estate agents have to move every five years, just so they know just how horrible it is. Plus, that would churn the inventory a little more, and that's good for all of us.

All that said, it's only natural that we downplay the downsides of doing a deal with us. Other professionals do it, too. Car salesmen don't emphasize how hard it will be to park that oversized SUV. Contractors don't highlight the joys of living through a home construction project. And lawyers bury the fine print in, well, literal fine print.

But painting a rosy scenario has the downside of making it look so easy that people are tempted to either do it on their own or hire the cheapest agent they can find—after all, why hire a top-notch professional for something simple like selling a home?

Instead, we need to show sellers just how hard it is to sell a home. We need to make it look complicated and complex, because the harder it is, the more likely that the client will realize that she needs someone really great at her job to guide her through it.

At my company, we came up with a visual way to express the challenges of buying and selling a home. We drew up what we called the "Journey," which was literally a pathway from "Consultation to Closing," showing all the stops along the way where our agents provided buyers and sellers with services. The point of the journey was to draw out all those steps to demonstrate just how much work we have to do to get a seller through the process.

The point is this: don't make it look easy. Make it clear that selling a home is hard, but that you're the agent who can get them through it.

7. Communication. Ensuring clear communication is important because it's necessary (but not sufficient) if you're going to provide a great service experience. That's why finding out how your clients want to be communicated with is one of the most important things you can do at that consultation. Some clients want phone calls. Some want texts. Some want a combination. Some will nominate a designated point person, and some will want you to conference all the clients in for any major discussions. Every client has different needs; it's your job to find out what they are.

The delineation of the Seven CORE Services can actually help you identify weaknesses in your own repertoire. Let's say, for example, that you think you're pretty good at representing sellers. Okay, maybe so. But realize that being great at the job of working with a seller means being great at providing all the specific services that they need: Counseling, Pricing, Staging, Marketing, Negotiation, Transaction Management, and Communication. Have you fully developed all those skills? If not, you can get better at your job, which is the whole point of CORE.

Presenting the Project Plan

Every agent is different and should present their value package in their own way. However you make that presentation, though, you should keep these guidelines in mind:

First, find ways to differentiate yourself. What makes you different? For every element of your Project Plan, you want to find some unique twist that makes your approach stand out. All the other agents in your market are going to go into that seller's living room and say that they have a website, that they syndicate, that they give great service. You need to find specific points that define you and your brokerage.

Ask yourself this question: "can my competitors say the same thing I'm saying?" If they could, you need to dig deeper to find a granular level of differentiation. For example, maybe you provide professional photography on every listing, or social media advertising, or some other feature other agents aren't utilizing. Or maybe you take the traditional open house and turn it into an "Event Open House" with calls to the neighborhood, direct mail, advertising—extras that other agents don't provide.

Who do you compare yourself to? Well, if you know who your potential sellers are meeting with, then make that straight broker-to-broker or agent-to-agent comparison. Never disrespect your competition, or talk them down, but make legitimate comparisons: "Oh, you're meeting with Basement Realty? They're a fine firm, but the big difference between us is that..."

And if you don't know who else your potential clients are meeting with, then it's a lot easier to find points of distinction. Just make your comparison to a made-up "Brand X" broker, an imaginary straw man who embodies all the mediocrity in your marketplace.

Indeed, articulating the Seven CORE Services individually helps you identify points of differentiation between you and the average agent. Again, we often broadly define the quality of our work—"I'm really good working with sellers!"—without explaining what that means you're good at:

- counseling your sellers to help them identify their specific, individualized needs;

- guiding them through the pricing process, and helping them set the best possible price for getting the home sold;

- detailing and staging the home for maximum effect;

- marketing the home both broadly and narrowly;

- negotiating their offer to get them the best deal;

- managing them through the challenging transactional process; and

- communicating with them clearly and effectively the entire time.

If you do all those things well, especially if you can find ways to quantify how you do them better than anyone else, you have a legitimate point of differentiation to help you in your marketing. Like, maybe it's tough to show how you're better than other agents at counseling or pricing, but you could try to find metrics that show you negotiate better deals for your sellers than the average agent.

Second, show, don't tell. You've heard this classic bit of presentation advice before: don't tell people what you're going to do, show them. So when you're reviewing the elements of your Project Plan, you need to use what we call "Showpieces," visual elements that illustrate the points of differentiation you're making.

For example, your standard showpieces should include your marketing collateral examples, before-and-after conditioning photos, market share graphs, and the beautiful listings that you'll pull up on your tablet. Indeed, your tablet is itself a showpiece, insofar as it communicates the message that you use technology effectively in servicing your clients' needs.

What qualifies as a showpiece? First, a showpiece should be seen, not read. Your client should be able to grasp the value of the showpiece just by looking at it or leafing through it. She shouldn't have to read it to understand it. Why? Because you don't want her reading while you're trying to make a presentation. If you have showpieces that need to be read, you should send them to the client either before the presentation in a pre-listing orientation package or use them as leave-behinds.

Second, a showpiece should look gorgeous. You should have high standards for anything you bring into a listing presentation. Don't bring in black-and-white photocopies—or even worse, copies of copies—of marketing collateral. Everything you show should be full-color and printed on good paper.

Finally, a showpiece should illustrate services you provide to address seller needs. A showpiece should be directly connected to a presentation point that you want to make as part of your Seven CORE Services. Before you include something in your presentation package, ask yourself, "does this piece address something that sellers need to know?" If it doesn't illustrate an important point you want to make, get rid of it. You don't need it muddying up your presentation.

Third, connect services to needs. A crucial way that you can differentiate yourself is to connect the services you offer to the value they provide your clients. A laundry list of marketing tools or website features is useless unless you make a connection between what you do and what your clients need.

For example, let's say that you want to talk about your fabulous website. Too many times, agents default to describing their marketing tools in the abstract, so when they discuss the website, they'll focus on how many hits they get or the features they provide. But that's not what's important to the seller. Make the connection: "our website is designed to generate eyeballs on your listing, and drive inquiries directly to me as the listing agent, who is the best person to answer those questions and, more importantly, get that buyer into your home."

Similarly, it's okay to talk about yourself, so long as you connect everything you're saying to the needs of the client. For example, let's say you want to make the point that you've been in business for over 20 years. That's terrific. Congratulations! But how is that important to the client? How is your long career responsive to your client's needs? Make that connection—talk about how you bring experience in the local area, that you know the inventory, that you've brought results to your past clients. Use your experience as validation to foster confidence in your client, to essentially communicate "you need someone who is capable of selling your home, and I have the track record to get the job done."

The key, though, is this: don't just talk about what you do or who you are—make the connection to how you're going to service your client's needs. That's what will make your Project Plan stand out.

Chapter 8

The Collaborative Pricing Process: Damn, Real Estate Agents!

I'VE HEARD IT. YOU'VE HEARD IT. WE'VE ALL HEARD IT.

Damn real estate agents! All they want to do is price it for a quick sale!

Remember when I told you about selling my penthouse condo? I listed it with Margo and Donna, two of my best agents, who deferred to me in setting the initial price, which, of course, led me to overprice it wildly. So it sat. And sat. And then after a while, they approached me about sitting down to go over "the marketing," which I knew, because I'm not totally stupid, actually meant that they were going to beat me up on the pricing. Which they did.

Now, I already told you the happy ending to the story: they showed me that I was overpriced, convinced me to make a correction, and we sold it a few weeks later.

Here's the part I didn't tell you about that "price correction" discussion. We sat at my dining table. They stacked up the evidence: the list of homes that buyers had purchased after seeing and rejecting my condo, the buyer and broker feedback, the market trends, all that. And at the end, they looked me in the eye and gave me a recommendation on price.

And here was my reaction, what went through my head:

Damn real estate agents! All they want to do is price it for a quick sale!

Now, here's what's interesting about that: I have had my license for over 30 years. I've been actively managing a real estate company for almost 20 years. And I've probably taught the fundamentals of pricing dozens and dozens of times to both clients and agents. I know how pricing works.

And on top of that, I knew those agents. I'd been working with them for years, liked them, trusted them, and should have known that they had my best interests at heart.

Yet, despite all that, I still had that little voice: "Damn real estate agents!"

In other words, no matter how knowledgeable I was about the subject, and no matter how much I liked my agents, I still had an almost reflexive and instinctive suspicion that they were trying to manipulate me on price. It was still there, like a little devil perched on my shoulder, jabbing at me with his pitchfork.

Luckily, I ignored that little demon, and listened to my agents. Because, a few weeks later, when the house sold, instead of:

Damn real estate agents!

It was:

Damn, real estate agents!

With a rueful smile, rather than a shaken fist.

Here's the point: if I wasn't immune to that impulse, then no one is. If I could have that negative reaction to an agent recommending a price I didn't like, then anyone can.

And that's why the traditional listing presentation's agent-centric approach, which asserts that clients should trust their agent as an all-knowing expert on pricing, and do whatever that agent says, is so wrong-headed. Because they don't. Sellers absolutely do not trust us on pricing. No matter how much they like us, they're invariably going to suspect, at least a little, that we're trying to underprice the home to get it sold and collect the commission as quickly as possible. So if your approach is to assume that sellers will blindly trust your expertise on price, without educating them about the process or explaining how pricing works, you're almost playing into that stereotype. It's almost a cliché that you should never trust someone who opens up with, "Trust me, I'm an expert!"

Another problem with this traditional approach is that it unnecessarily puts the burden on the agent to own the price. If you're the one suggesting a price, then you're the one who has to defend it.

Why take that on? You're not setting the price; the market is setting the price. Indeed, you're putting yourself in an adversarial position to your client, when you're supposed to be on her side. How many times have you ended up basically negotiating with your clients on price, trying to get them to make concessions that you know they need if they want to get sold? You did that to yourself, because you put yourself on one side of the debate and them on the other.

On top of all that, you've chosen to be the bearer of bad tidings, almost always a source of disappointment to sellers fervently hoping for a higher price. You almost never get that happy day when your sellers are overjoyed to find out that their home is worth twice what they thought.

Yay! You're a hero!

Instead, you're almost always in the unenviable position of dashing your clients' unrealistic expectations of the massive windfall that Zillow promised them.

Boo! You're the worst!

You don't need to do it that way. You don't need to take the agent-oriented approach to pricing that posits you as some "all-knowing expert" demanding absolute trust and obedience. Instead, you should take the more client-oriented approach of focusing on (1) educating your clients about the pricing process, (2) elaborating and explaining the market environment, and then (3) collaborating with them on setting the best price possible that will still get the home sold.

Educate

First, we need to educate the sellers about how to price their home. We often assume that clients understand the fundamentals of why comparable properties are so important, or what constitutes a "comp," so we just launch into our CMA without giving them the grounding in the fundamentals. But many of our sellers have never actually sold a home, and a lot of the others haven't done it in a long time.

So you should always be prepared to explain the core principles of the pricing process:

1. *You price a home based on comparable properties.* Pricing is very straightforward: you value a home compared to the price of similar homes in the same local area. Why? Because once a listing is on

the market, buyers are going to be able to compare it to those other properties, not just the ones for sale but the ones that have recently sold. And they're going to buy the one that they think provides the best value.

Sellers can't hide from the comps. Buyers usually have easy access to the entire MLS—every home that is on the market in your local area. Any buyer can pull up a real estate website on her laptop, run a search, and get all the information she needs about every home that's for sale. And buyers can even get access, usually through their agents, to information on all recent sales in that market.

In other words, you need to explain to your sellers that they can't ignore the comps, because the buyers won't.

2. *The most important comps are the solds, not the unsolds.* Once you've established that pricing a home depends on the "comps," then it's important to define what types of comps are most important. Specifically, sellers need to understand the importance of pricing to the sold properties, not the unsold, "active" listings.

Indeed, you should strike the word "active" from your vocabulary. Homes on the market aren't "active." There's nothing "active" about them. They're just sitting, doing nothing, inert, motionless. Call them what they are: the unsold homes. Unsold. Unwanted. Unloved. Untouched.

Price to the solds, not the unsolds. The logic seems simple, right? After all, if you're trying to get your home sold, you price to the solds. If instead you price to the homes that are unsold, you're likely to join them.

But sellers tend to focus on the prices of the unsold homes. For one thing, the unsold prices are almost always higher, and sellers obviously like that. But the bigger problem is that your sellers get a preconception about what their home is worth when they start looking on their own, usually by doing a simple inventory search on a real estate website. They never see the solds, just the unsolds. So they come into your meeting having only seen the "asking price" of the unsold homes that are for sale, which gives them an inflated view of what's happening in the market. But those "active" homes haven't sold! Why would we want to price at their level?

So your sellers need to understand that when they're looking at comps, they should prioritize the sold properties, not the ones that still haven't sold. Unsold listings are part of the CMA because they represent the competition, and you need to know what you're up against, but they shouldn't be the basis of setting your price range.

3. *You select sold "comps" based on location, size, and style.* Most people have heard the old joke that the price of a home comes down to three things: Location, Location, and Location. Isn't that hilarious? Real estate humor is the best!

Of course, it's mostly true. The most important driver of real estate value is the location of the property. So when you're picking comps, you start by looking at the homes in the immediate area.

But while location is the most important factor, it's not the only one. You also have to look for homes that are similarly sized in terms of the overall square footage, number of bedrooms and bathrooms, lot size, and things like that. And then once you've found your nearby, similarly-sized homes, you prioritize the homes with a similar style: if the home is a colonial, other colonials are better comps than, say, a raised ranch or a contemporary.

So your sellers need to understand that when you're choosing comps, you're going to focus first on location as the single most important driver of price. And then once you've found homes in the local area, you'll narrow down on the ones of similar size and style. That's how you establish your price range: start with location, narrow down with size and style.

4. *You then adjust within your price range for condition and amenities.* Once you've established a price range using your comps, you have to adjust within that price range for distinguishing amenities between your listing and the comparable sales. This is the real nitty-gritty of the comparative market analysis: the home-by-home comparison between properties to determine relative value.

Unfortunately, sellers always overvalue their amenities. They think that their granite countertops put them in a different price range from the seller down the street. I once had a seller tell me that his home was worth $300,000 more than his competition, because he had a sauna. A used sauna. With all his sweat already in it. Meanwhile, a buyer could purchase that other house, which was virtually identical, and put in a sauna for about $25,000. Kind of a better deal, right?

Sellers need to understand: amenities don't change your price range, just where you fall within it. Specifically, they can help you make meaningful comparisons to narrow down your pricing: this property is similarly-sized, but it's on a cul-de-sac; that one has a finished basement that doesn't show up in the square footage; this one was just renovated; that one has a pool.

The same goes for condition. You want your listing to be immaculately staged and detailed, and in fantastic showing condition, because that makes it easier to sell and gets you the best price possible in your range. But it generally doesn't change the range that you're in.

You need to explain that every home is different, and every difference has a small but meaningful impact on the valuation. That's why you go through each of those properties in the CMA, so you can make those granular comparisons.

5. *Ultimately, the market sets the price.* Finally, your sellers need to make sure that they listen to the market: "You don't set the price, and I don't set the price—the market sets the price."

What do we mean by that? Well, too often, sellers price their home based on other considerations having nothing to do with what the market is telling them:

- *Pricing on need.* Many sellers will simply price based on what they need to get into their next home, without understanding that buyers simply do not care. Just ask your clients, "when you buy your next home, are you going to care what the sellers 'need' for their next purchase?"

- *Pricing on improvements.* Sellers always think that they're going to earn back 100% of every dollar they put into their house. If they bought it for $400,000, and put in a $50,000 kitchen, they think it's worth at least $450,000. You need to explain to them that it doesn't work that way: homes appreciate, but the stuff in them depreciates. That high-end refrigerator they put in started losing value the minute they plugged it in. Get them the annual "Cost vs. Value Report" from *Remodeling Magazine*, which usually shows how most home improvement projects return 50-75 cents on the dollar.

- *Pricing on a Zestimate.* Some sellers will want to price their home based entirely on the Zestimate, ignoring an agent's CMA or their own analysis of the market. Of course, they'll only show you the Zestimate if it's way above market value–they never seem to bring up the Zestimate if it comes in low. How do you handle that? Well, try going online and searching for "Spencer Rascoff sold his home for less than the Zestimate," and find all the articles reporting on how the founder of Zillow sold his house for 40% below his own website's evaluation. Spencer has been admirably candid and forthright about admitting that the Zestimate is not perfect, and that sellers should listen to the advice of their agents in pricing their home. So print a few of those articles, and keep them handy in your briefcase.

Your sellers need to understand: none of that matters. What matters is the market. Your role in the CMA process is not to "set the price," but to help them understand what the market is telling them.

Elaborate: The AVM and the CMA

Once your clients understand pricing fundamentals, you can start digging into the details of the current market environment.

Now, the traditional advice is for agents to whip out their CMA and start exploring the comps. That's fine, I guess. But I have an alternative, somewhat contrarian suggestion: start by reviewing the AVMs.

What's the AVM? If you're not familiar with the term, an AVM is an "Automated Valuation Model," a tool that provides real estate valuations using mathematical modeling. Zillow's Zestimate was the first popularly available AVM, but you can now find AVMs on many broker websites, and most real estate portals.

I'm surprised that most agents still do pricing presentations without referencing any of the AVMs that are available to them. If I went back in time and told an agent in 1995 that she could have access to a half-dozen automated appraisals of her listing to help her price a home, she'd jump at that chance. She'd be thrilled to have that kind of resource. Even today, most agents love pricing a home with a recent appraisal, simply because it gives them a new data point to consider in their own analysis.

But most agents still think of AVMs as a threat. They're stuck in that defensive mindset that the Zestimate is an intrusion on their professional responsibilities, that AVMs devalue the hard work that goes into making an on-the-ground market analysis. And agents resent the AVM because they're often terribly inaccurate, forcing agents to explain to sellers why they shouldn't price their home on a way-too-high AVM, and to buyers why they shouldn't make a ridiculous lowball offer on a way-too-low AVM.

We all need to get over that. AVMs are not a substitute for a CMA; they're a complement to the CMA. They're a resource that informs a proper market analysis. And agents make a mistake when they treat AVMs as the enemy, as a rival to be ignored or disparaged. Instead, agents should think of AVMs as a tool, among many tools, that can help them establish and explain the value of a home.

Indeed, a modern CMA has to account for automated valuations. After all, most of those AVMs are publicly available, and a resourceful seller is going to find them herself. You might as well confront them head-on, showing how some of them are consistent with your views, and why the inconsistent ones are off. And presenting an AVM that establishes the actual pricing environment can be a great way of allowing someone else to be the bearer of bad news for that seller. The AVM is a faceless, neutral, objective arbiter of value. That's not us saying that the home's value is 20% below what the seller hoped— it's the robot! Let the robot take the heat.

And you have so many AVMs available to you that you can be selective in the ones you highlight: RPR, Zillow, Trulia, Realtor.com, Cyberhomes.com, Eppraisal.com, Realestate.com, Homegain.com, and any number of other sites. You also might have access to some private AVMs through your broker or other professional networks. You don't need all of them, so pick the best ones, the ones that you think accurately reflect the market value, the same way that you pick the best comps when you're doing your CMA.

Then, when you sit down to go over the market, start with the AVMs. Explain what they are, why they're useful, and also why they're no substitute for a professional CMA. And once you're done with the AVMs, pull out your CMA, say, "Okay, let's find out what the market is *really* telling us," and then start elaborating and filling in the gaps for the information that's in it. Don't just give it to them and expect that they'll understand it. You have to go over it with them and point out all the similarities and differences between their home and the comparable properties.

Here are just a couple of suggestions for delivering your CMA to your client:

1. *Start with the solds.* I am amazed at how many CMA tools start with the unsold listings. That makes no sense. First impressions matter, so if you start with the unsold listings you're going to anchor your sellers to think that those prices are realistic. They're not. That's why those properties haven't sold. So start with the sold properties, which will anchor your client in reality and help frame the rest of your discussion.

2. *Have copies ready.* Always make a copy for your client, and a copy for you, and bind them with a clip rather than a staple so that they can be separated out. I know that the modern trend is to provide CMAs on a tablet, and that's fine. But you always want to have copies handy, because pricing can be almost a tactile experience. Clients like to spread the comps out in front of them and look at them all together. Don't rob them of that experience because you want to impress them with the fancy bells and whistles of your online CMA.

3. *Go see the comps.* You should know the properties in your CMA. I'm amazed at how many agents will present a CMA with listings that they've never seen, or know nothing about, other than what's contained on the MLS sheet. If you can't see the properties, drive by. If you can't drive by, then call the listing agent and ask some questions. If you can't call the listing agent, then I don't know what you do. Just call the listing agent, okay? You can't present a CMA of properties that you don't know.

4. *Find something to say about each comp.* If you're including that listing in your CMA, you need a reason. Find some angle of comparison. Maybe it's smaller. Maybe it's got nicer amenities. Maybe it's under a high-tension wire. Whatever it is, have something useful to contribute to the discussion that's not obvious from the listing information itself.

5. *Have "non-comps" ready.* When you're working on your CMA, you're going to come across properties that aren't really comparable, even though your seller would love to use them as a comp because they establish a much higher price point. But, in your opinion, that sale is not a good comp: maybe it's a lot larger, or in a different school district, or has a different level of amenities. That's fine. But print out that comp anyway, put it aside, and have it available in case your client brings it up. If he raises it to protest the choices of comps that you did select, you want to demonstrate that you considered and rejected it for a good reason.

6. *Finally, don't be afraid of silence.* Sellers sometimes need time to come to grips with the realities of what the CMA is telling them. They might need time to study the comps, and get used to the idea that their home is worth less than they thought. Give them that time. Don't rush them, and don't feel a need to fill the silence with chitter-chatter.

Collaborate

You're going to take a collaborative approach to figuring out the asking price for that home. Instead of being agent-oriented, telling the sellers what they should do, you're going to be client-oriented by investing them in the decision-making process.

Why is collaborative pricing more effective? First, engaging them in setting a price invests them in the decision. When you announce the price from up on high as the "expert," you're treating them like a subordinate. But when you collaborate with them, you're treating them like a partner in the decision-making process. And that's the way it should be. Your job is to guide them to a decision, not make it for them.

Second, asking them what they think puts the obligation on them to defend their choices. If you've set up your CMA correctly, then you've established an unspoken price range that should be obvious to the sellers. But if they decide to go outside that range, and suggest a dramatically higher price, it's now on them to defend their price. You no longer own the price, they do.

Third, asking their opinion respects their authority as the owner of the property. Ultimately, it's their decision, isn't it? Shouldn't they bear some of the responsibility for setting that price, rather than shunting it over to you? Ultimately, it's their home, their choice. They're the boss.

So here's what you say:

Okay, now that we've gone over the CMA, what do we think is a good price range for our listing? We have these properties that have sold at these prices, and over here we have some competing unsold properties that are still on the market. What do you think is a good price?

Then let them think about it. Again, don't be afraid of the silence, and don't feel a compulsion to fill the space.

At that point, one of three things is going to happen:

1. *They'll refuse to make any suggestions.* Whether it's because they think it's your job to give your opinion, or because they're embarrassed to present the price they really want, they might throw the question back to you. That's fine. Just do what you normally do: point out the sold comps, and suggest a range based on them. But think about how the dynamic has changed. You gave them the opportunity to suggest a price, and they turned you down. Instead, they literally asked you to suggest a price. That's a very different situation from the typical "trust me I'm the expert" situation. Essentially, they gave you permission to make your recommendation. You're still being client-oriented: you're complying with their request.

2. *They'll suggest a price that's way too high.* Ah well, the collaborative process didn't really work—they still want to overprice their home. But the dynamic is completely reversed. Now, the responsibility is on them to justify that unrealistic price, in the same way that the traditional pricing presentation puts the obligation on you to defend a realistic price. Essentially, you're now the one making a pricing objection, rather than the seller. You've completely flipped the dynamic.

3. *They'll suggest a price within the reasonable range.* Hey, it happens! Once you've recovered from your shock and picked yourself up off the floor, just agree with them, fill in that price in your listing agreement, and move on. Happy day!

This CORE collaborative approach to pricing is simply a much better way of guiding sellers through the process. Instead of being the bearer of bad news, you're going to help the seller discover reality for herself. And instead of taking ownership of the price, you're going to let the market speak for itself. You're still the expert, but in the CORE approach your expertise is designed to guide the seller through the pricing decision, not make that decision for her.

Now, I'm not saying that this approach is going to solve all your pricing problems. You're still going to have sellers (like me) who are going to insist on overpricing their listing, despite what the market is telling them. And that's okay. Sellers who overprice their listing aren't bad people, or crazy, or trying to be difficult. They're just overly optimistic about their chances of getting a windfall on the sale of their home. If they want to test the market, they have that right. They're the client, it's their call.

Similarly, you shouldn't be ashamed if you occasionally take an overpriced listing. Maybe you feel like you have to work with that client because of a personal relationship, or you really don't want to give up a listing in your farm. Or maybe you think that the sellers will be more realistic once they get a response from the market. You might have plenty of good reasons to take an overpriced listing.

I don't understand the "shaming" that I sometimes see on tour, where agents will "tsk tsk" about how a particular home is too high, as if they've never taken an overpriced listing. Everyone has taken overpriced listings. Everyone. You just don't want to make a habit of it.

Chapter 9

The Buyer Consultation: No, We Didn't Forget...

WE ALWAYS GIVE SHORT SHRIFT TO BUYERS, DON'T WE?

Sellers get a full-blown presentation, with glossy materials and a CMA and all that.

Buyers? We meet them at the house with a printout from the MLS.

Sellers sign an exclusive agreement where we guarantee a range of services and secure our right to get paid when we're successful.

Buyers? We don't ask them to sign anything.

And sellers get all the attention when we talk about the "client consultation." Three whole chapters.

Buyers? They get this measly little afterthought.

It's degrading!

We need to start treating buyers the way we treat sellers. Great real estate agents should sign every buyer to a representation agreement that provides for exclusivity and a guaranteed suite of services. And part of that process should include a fully-realized consultative presentation, not just a hasty meeting outside the random listing that the buyer called them on.

Why don't we? Maybe it's because buyer agency is still relatively new. Until about 30 years ago, in most of the country, no one ever represented buyers in a fiduciary capacity, so all the systems that we developed during the formative years of the modern industry focused on sellers. That's why you'll almost never see a non-exclusive listing agreement anymore, but you'll still find agents working with buyers without any kind of legal protections at all.

Go back to the CORE Formula: think expansively about what buyers need at that first meeting, then creatively about how to satisfy that need, and then execute.

What do they need? They absolutely, positively, need to meet with you, and have a substantive discussion where you assess their needs, present your services, and review their financial profile. You can't possibly do good work for them if you barely know them.

The biggest challenge, of course, is that many buyers simply want to meet you at the home they called you on. Don't do that. Here's why:

- *It's unprofessional.* I once asked my dad, the doctor, why he didn't make "house calls," and he told me it was because he couldn't help his patients at their homes—he didn't have access to any of his necessary instruments. It's the same for you: you can't do your job if you make a "house call" for a buyer that you've never met. You don't know what she needs, and she doesn't know what you can do for her. So make it a rule that you consult with every buyer before you take them out.

- *It's dangerous.* I don't think I need to justify this. We all know the tragic stories of agents who have been killed showing properties to strangers. It's simply not safe. Even if your broker doesn't have a rule against it, set your own standards: you don't take anyone to see a home that you haven't met first and gotten some information from. Ideally, you should photocopy or scan a driver's license and send it to your office administrator for safe-keeping.

- *It's not fair for the seller.* You're supposed to be screening people before you let them into someone else's home. You have no idea whether you're giving access to some klepto who's going to start stuffing his pockets with silverware.

What if they refuse to meet with you beforehand? You're supposed to be good at persuading people, so convince them otherwise:

> *I appreciate that you want to meet at the house, but I'm afraid that I wouldn't be a very good agent if I didn't take a few minutes to at least get to know you a bit before we go look at a home. We only need about 15 minutes, but, in that time, I can find out what you're looking for, and I might have some other suggestions for properties that we could go see. I promise that you won't be*

wasting your time, because I'll be much better able to help you out if I know something about what you're looking for.

So let's meet at this diner, it's about five minutes away from the house.

If that doesn't work, stress that it's your company's policy (it should be!) that you never meet with someone you don't know at a listing. And if that doesn't work, go do something else and stop wasting your time on people who don't respect your professionalism.

So assuming you do convince them to meet with you, what should this consultation look like? Like the listing presentation, the buyer presentation has three parts: (1) the Needs Consultation, (2) the Project Plan, and (3) the Qualification Analysis. You see what we did there? It's the same layout as the listing presentation, except that you're going to provide the prequalification service in place of the Market Analysis.

The Needs Consultation. We provide the Needs Consultation in the same way and for the same reasons as we do for sellers: it's a great way to build rapport, get to know the client's familiarity with the process, and establish trust. And you should be asking the same kinds of questions:

- *Motivation.* Ask about their personal situation: why they are moving, how long have they been looking, and how quickly do they need to move?

- *Process.* Probe their understanding of the home-buying process and identify any concerns they might have.

- *Dream Home.* Get them to describe their "dream home," so that you can get a sense of what they're looking for. Where is it? What sized home do they need? Have they seen something they liked, and why? What are the "must have" and "can't have" features? This should be the heart of the consultation, because you really need to get to know their wants and needs.

- *Communication.* Find out how they want you to communicate with them: personal visits, calls, texts, emails, or what?

- *Expectations.* And, just like with sellers, you absolutely have to establish what they expect from an agent. You need to ask questions about their past experiences with service profession-als, so you can get a sense of what they like and don't like.

And, of course, throughout the Needs Consultation, you should be listening actively, asking follow-up questions, and taking notes to show that you're paying attention.

The Project Plan. Just like with sellers, you have a Project Plan that you can present to your buyers. The services are a little differ-ent, of course, since they're oriented to the needs of buyers, but you do have a lot of overlap:

1. *Consultation.* Just like with sellers, you're going to go through that consultation process, identifying needs and figuring out how to best service them.

2. *Qualifying.* Similar to the pricing service you provide sellers to help them avoid wasting time on the market with an overpriced listing, Qualifying is a financial service that is vital to ensuring that your buyers don't waste their time looking at homes they cannot afford.

3. *Searching.* Once you've qualified your buyer, your most sig-nificant responsibility is the search and screening process. You need to set up online searches, update them regularly, keep an eye out for FSBOs, and guide your buyers as they "shop" for a new home.

4. *Showing.* You're going to accompany them on showings to get to know their likes and dislikes, as you narrow down their "dream home" needs.

5. *Negotiation.* With buyers, you're on the other side of that negotiation process, helping them prepare a strategy and acting as their intermediary.

6. *Transaction Management.* Transaction management for buyers is even more important than for sellers, since buyers have to navigate the minefield of the mortgage process.

7. *Communication.* And, of course, throughout the entire process, you're going to communicate with them in their preferred method.

Moreover, you're going to present all of these services with Showpieces that illustrate your points of differentiation, connecting your services to the needs of your buyer.

Qualification Analysis. In the same way that you provide your Pricing Analysis to sellers at that initial consultation, you're going to provide your Qualifying services to your buyers to help determine their buying power. The Qualifying discussion with buyers is just as important as the pricing discussion with sellers. You don't want to waste their time (or yours) looking at homes that they cannot afford.

So why is it that every agent provides pricing to sellers, but defers qualifying to mortgage professionals? It can't be because qualifying is too complicated. Any agent can learn the fundamentals of determining a price range based on the borrower's financial profile and the prevailing interest rate. If you don't know how to do that, learn it. Yes, of course, you should always turn to a lender to get a formal pre-qualification or pre-approval letter, and you should probably get a loan officer opinion if your buyer has a complicated situation. But in most cases, a good real estate agent is fully capable of helping pre-qualify a buyer's price range. So do it.

So how do you qualify your buyer? You're not a mortgage lender, but you should know the two basic rules of thumb for determining a buyer's price range:

- *The 3.5x income rule.* Take the combined pre-tax income and multiply it by 3.5 to determine how much home the average client can afford. So if your married buyers together make $100,000, they can afford a home priced at about $350,000. (This used to be the 3x rule, but rates are a lot lower now than they were when the rule was created).

- *The ¼ income rule.* Conversely, if you want to focus on the monthly payment, take one-quarter of the client's monthly income—that's how about much she can spend on her monthly mortgage payment. So those same buyers making $100,000 a year earn about \$9,200 per month, and 1/4 of that is about \$2,300—the monthly payment they can support.

Both of these rules assume that your client can come up with a reasonable down payment, has decent credit, and all that. And the rules of thumb are not substitutes for a proper prequalification letter by a reliable lender. They're basically "meatball surgery." But they can at least get you through an initial showing appointment when you have no other options.

SEVEN CORE SERVICES

STAGE	SELLERS	BUYERS
COUNSELING	PROVIDE ADVICE FROM THE INITIAL CONSULTATION THROUGH THE FINAL CLOSING.	
FINANCIAL	**PRICING:** HELP SELLERS PRICE THE HOME ACCORDING TO MARKET CONDITIONS.	**QUALIFICATION:** HELP BUYERS GET PREQUALIFIED, AND EXPLAIN THE MORTGAGE PROCESS.
PREPARATION	**STAGING:** HELP SELLERS PREPARE THE HOME FOR SHOWINGS.	**SCREENING:** HELP BUYERS SORT THROUGH THE INVENTORY, AND SET UP SEARCHES.
ON/IN THE MARKET	**MARKETING:** MARKET THE HOME BROADLY AND NARROWLY.	**SHOWING:** ORGANIZE AND MANAGE THE SHOWING PROCESS.
NEGOTIATION	HANDLE ALL OFFERS AND NEGOTIATE THE BEST POSSIBLE TERMS.	
PROJECT MANAGEMENT	MANAGE THE TRANSACTION FROM ACCEPTED OFFER THROUGH THE INSPECTION, MORTGAGE, TITLE WALK-THROUGH, AND CLOSING PROCESS.	
COMMUNICATION	PROVIDE THE CLIENT WITH A CLEAR, CONSTANT, AND COMPREHENSIVE STREAM OF UPDATES.	

Part Two Conclusion: Be Great at Your Job

THE KEY TO A PERSUASIVE CLIENT PRESENTATION IS NOT only being great at your job, but believing you're great at your job.

Here's what I mean. If you're great at your job, the presentation is a lot easier, because you can point to all the physical manifestations of your commitment to an amazing client service experience:

- Client testimonials that attest to the quality of your work;

- Online reviews that aggregate and quantify your clients' experiences;

- Performance stats that measure metrics like your listing success rate, days-on-market, listing retention, or anything else that shows how well you do your job on the listing side. And on your buyer side, how about a measure of your average listing discount off the last listed price, as a measure of your negotiating ability?

- Physical manifestations of your commitment to getting things right, like service checklists and guides;

- Live demonstrations, like pulling out your tablet and showing the beautiful marketing you provide for your current listings, or video testimonials from your recent buyers;

The more evidence you have about the quality of your work, the easier it becomes to make the case that this client is making the right choice in hiring you.

But you also need to *believe* you're great at your job, the job of helping people buy and sell real estate. Because if you believe that you're great, then you'll have the confidence to go into every presentation and assert those qualifications. You won't shy away and you won't be tempted to rely on clichés and crutches when you present your value proposition. You'll be able to speak openly and honestly.

And, most importantly, everything you say about why they should hire you will be true.

Part Three:
Client Management

Chapter 10

What People Need: Getting to Delight

LET'S PLAY "FILL-IN-THE-BLANK."

You ready?

Okay, just write down the first word that comes to mind when you read this sentence:

"I just started working with a new client, and she needs a lot of help, because she's a first-time home-_____."

You fill in that blank? Okay, great!

So what'd you put?

You put "buyer," didn't you? As in "first-time home-buyer"?

Of course you did! It's okay. That's what everyone puts. I've done this exercise with lots of agents over the years, and they all answer "first-time home-buyer."

No one ever says, "first-time home-seller." It's not a term that we use in the real estate industry. It even sounds a little strange when you say it out loud, like your mouth just can't get around the words.

"First-time home-seller."

"First-time home-seller."

"First-time home-seller."

It just sounds wrong.

Why is that? Why do we have like a zillion marketing pieces and programs and systems designed for first-time home-buyers, and nothing for first-time home-sellers? Why do we think of first-time home-buyers as these timid little birds that we have to coddle and pamper with all this hand-holding, and we think of first-time home-sellers as... well... sellers? Just like every other seller.

Part of it is that we just wrongly think that anyone who owns a home is an experienced client. After all, homeowners obviously went through the transactional process when they bought the house, so they're no longer a "first-timer." They already lost their virginity. But is that really true? You go through the transactional process every day; is it the same process for buyers as for sellers? Is the act of searching, going on showings, and getting a mortgage the same as pricing, staging, and marketing your home? Do buyers and sellers have the same set of expectations, hopes, fears, or anxieties?

Of course not! Buying and selling are totally different experiences. So someone who has already bought a home knows virtually nothing about the challenges of selling that home. And yet, we have no specialized concept of a first-time home-seller as someone who needs a higher degree of care than an experienced seller, who might need more education about the process, more guidance about staging, more hand-holding through the showings.

In other words, we basically treat our sellers like they're all the same. Other than that narrow exception we make for first-time home-buyers, we don't think of our clients as having specialized needs that require customized solutions. Instead, we provide a cookie-cutter approach to standardized service with the same scripts, the same materials, the same programs.

Take, for example, the standard one-size-fits-all listing presentation that we've taught agents to give to sellers. They visit the home, they take a tour, and then they start giving their prepared set of scripts and dialogues designed to convince the seller to list with them. It's the same presentation every time. Every time.

But if you've been in the business for a while, you know every seller is different. Some of them are afraid, some are enthusiastic. Some want to be involved in decision-making, some want to defer to their agent. Some want constant attention, and some don't want to be bothered until you get an offer. Some know what to expect from the process, and some are complete neophytes. But you're never going to discover what makes a particular client unique if you take a one-size-fits-all approach to servicing them.

And that's the real problem: our mindset. The fact that we've never even identified the concept of a "first-time home-seller" is a red flag that, as an industry, we're thinking too narrowly about what our clients need from us. We've already seen this in how we thought too narrowly about a homeowner's need to know how much her home was worth, leaving an opening for Zillow to service that need and supplant our role as the authority on home values. And thought too narrowly about our clients' needs for vendor referrals, opening the door to companies like Angie's List and HomeAdvisor to take over that category.

Again and again, when I look at the real estate industry, I see missed opportunities where we've neglected the needs of our clients, or the people we wish would be our clients. Take, for example, all our real estate websites. Real estate came to the internet over 20 years ago, when we first started putting inventory online and allowing people to search for homes on their own. Over the years, we've collectively invested millions of dollars into those websites, and seen third-party companies like Zillow and Trulia put millions more into their portals. And all our sites get better every year, with bells and whistles like high-resolution photos, videos, 3D walkthroughs, mapping, school reports, community information, and all the rest.

But those sites are not built around the needs of our actual clients. They're not built for our sellers, or our active buyers, or even non-transactional clients like homeowners. Rather, our sites are optimized for shoppers: people who are thinking about buying but aren't yet working with an agent. They're designed almost exclusively to attract shoppers with all the bells and whistles, and then induce them to click on the "Find out More!" button to convert them to a lead. As usual, we put our energies and creativity into generating leads, not servicing the needs of our clients. Leads, not needs.

For example, we don't build our websites for listed sellers. Yes, we do provide a valuable service for sellers on our sites, just by listing their property online so the shoppers can see it. But why would a seller even go onto one of our real estate sites herself, other than to look to see whether her listing is up (and heaven help you if it isn't)? We don't have any tools for her there, no services, no information. Indeed, when you initiate a relationship with a company—shopping sites, banks, airlines, etc.—the first thing you usually get is an account on their website with a login and a password. But not in real estate. Not for sellers. They don't need a login for their broker's website, because the site doesn't have any tools that are customized for their listing.

This is a perfect example of how our narrow perspective of what people need prevents us from providing a better experience for our clients. So instead, just as an exercise, let's follow the CORE Formula, and think expansively about some of the things sellers might need from a website during the course of their transaction, from the day they list until the day they close:

- videos and tutorials explaining the staging process,

- links to visit their listing on all the major portals,

- dynamic reports on the online traffic to their listing on all those sites and portals,

- periodic market updates, with statistics on sales, prices, etc.,

- a "live CMA" with real-time online updates on comparable properties: new competitor listings, sales, price changes, etc.,

- a "report" button to let their agent (or administrative staff) know about any problems,

- a communication platform (i.e., like Slack) for tracking and storing messages with their agent,

- a calendar displaying all their showings and other appointments (inspection, closing, etc.), linked to their own personal calendars,

- written feedback on showings from buyers and buyer agents,

- a document repository containing PDFs of all the paperwork relating to their listing and transaction, along with links to their digital documents executed by e-signature,

- updated "to-do" lists tracking the progress of their transaction,

- links to recommended vendors to help with the sales and moving process.

You see what I mean? If we thought expansively about the needs of our sellers when we built our websites, we would add all those features. But we think narrowly, so instead we build our websites almost exclusively for the short-term sugar rush of an online lead.

Imagine, though, that you had that type of website, or an app that did the same thing. Wouldn't that do a lot more for our business than more low-percentage online leads? Wouldn't you have a tremendous advantage in every listing presentation when you showed sellers all the ways you'd be servicing their needs with your website? Wouldn't you provide a better experience, which would generate evangelical clients who would rave about you to all their friends? And wouldn't your job be a lot easier if all that information was provided automatically, rather than requiring you to do everything yourself, freeing up time to do even more client development work?

That's the whole point of CORE: doing good work for the client, providing a better experience, is not just good for the client. It's good for the agent.

Getting to Delight

Let's go back to the CORE Formula, which starts with a simple instruction: think expansively about what people need. So let's break down what clients need from us when they come to us to help them buy or sell a home:

First, they need us to close their deal. This is what our clients need at the most fundamental level. If they're sellers, they need us to sell the home. If we get it sold, we've done the job. If we didn't, we didn't. Same with buyers: at the very least, we need to get them in their new home.

But that simplicity can be a little misleading. You can get the house sold and still not fully address your client's needs. Maybe you didn't price the home correctly, and it chased the market for months, ultimately selling for less than it could have with a proper pricing strategy. Maybe you didn't stage the home well, which probably meant more time on the market and a lower selling price. After all, we all know agents who manage to sell a few homes a year even though they have no idea what they're doing. Sometimes, the home sells itself, not because of the agent, but despite her.

So we can't say that the only thing our clients need is to get the deal done. That's necessary, but not sufficient.

Second, they need to get the best possible terms. Now, we start to get into the qualitative nature of the experience. It's not just closing the deal, it's about getting a good deal.

Let's say you're working with a seller. You priced it well, staged it carefully, marketed it aggressively, negotiated well, and got the seller the best possible price in a reasonable amount of time. In other words, you didn't just get the home sold, but you got good results.

Or if you were working with a buyer, you helped them quickly determine their purchasing power and identify their wants and needs in a home. Then you negotiated a good deal: the right price, closing date, all the other terms.

Is that enough? For most people, yes, that's probably sufficient: you got the deal closed, you got a good price, you closed in a reasonable amount of time.

But following the CORE Formula, you have to think even more expansively about what people need from you. You're not just going to get the home sold, and you're not just going to get the best possible terms. You're going to do something else, something even more important, something that's going to set you apart from the other people in your industry.

Third, they need a great experience throughout the process. That's more than just getting the house sold or getting the right price. Real estate transactions are complex and difficult. You have to work closely with those clients for a long period of time, guiding them through a series of difficult challenges from their initial consultation through their final closing. Your ability to manage those clients through that process makes an enormous difference in the experience they ultimately have.

For example, let's say you worked with a seller through a difficult transaction. It could have gone bad in a dozen ways. But you prepared them for the process at your initial consultation, so they knew what to expect and were never surprised when complications came up. You explained what they needed to do at every stage of the deal, so they always felt they were in control of the situation. You counseled them when they experienced challenges, so they never got too frustrated. And you demonstrated your mastery throughout the process, so they always felt confident that you were taking great care of them. That's not just getting the deal done, or getting the right terms, it's about giving a great experience.

Ultimately, that's what your clients really need from you: get the home sold, get the best possible results, and provide them with a wonderful experience through the whole process. And it's the same for buyers: find them the right home, on the best possible terms, and give them a great experience. Only if you do all that can you say that you've truly satisfied their needs.

This is what we're going to call the Three Levels of Client Needs:

- *Level One: Completion.* You got the job done.

- *Level Two: Success.* You got the job done and delivered good results.

- *Level Three: Delight.* You got the job done, delivered good results, and provided a qualitatively great experience during the process.

You see how that works? If we're going to think expansively about what our transactional clients need, and the services we can provide to them, we have to go beyond simply defining our service as "getting the home sold." That's necessary, but not sufficient. You also have to get the right results, and focus on the qualitative nature of the experience.

You can see this dynamic play out in any service experience, from any type of provider. Let's say, for example, that you have a toothache, so you go to visit your dentist. You obviously want the dentist to stop the tooth from hurting—i.e., Level One "Completion." And you also want the dentist to provide the treatment as efficiently as possible—i.e., Level Two "Success."

But is that all you want? Wouldn't you also hope for a dentist who is up-to-date with the state-of-the-art technology for her profession, to make sure you're getting the best possible treatment? Who will minimize the painfulness of the procedure? Who will talk you through the process, so you know what's going on? Even on the most prosaic level, don't you want a dentist who doesn't keep you sitting for an hour in the waiting room? All those things go into the quality of the experience you're going to have as a patient.

That's exactly what we have to do as real estate agents: get our clients to delight.

So how do we do that? Well, now that we've thought expansively about what our clients need, let's think creatively about how to get it for them.

Three Levels of Client Needs

Professional	Level 1: Completion *You got the job done.*	Level 2: Success *You got the job done, with great results.*	Level 3: Delight *ALSO: you provided a pleasurable experience during the transaction.*
Real Estate Agent	You sold the house.	ALSO: you sold the house quickly and for the best possible price in that market.	ALSO: you flawlessly managed the complex transactional process.
Doctor	You successfully cured the illness.	ALSO: you quickly diagnosed the illness and cured it efficiently with a minimum of discomfort.	ALSO: you counseled the patient through a difficult and painful treatment with a soothing bedside manner.
Plumber	You fixed the leak.	ALSO: you fixed the leak quickly and on budget.	ALSO: you took extra time to explain what went wrong and how to prevent it from happening again.
Hair Stylist	You gave a nice haircut.	ALSO: you gave a beautiful haircut that looked just like the model in the magazine photo the customer brought in.	ALSO: you provided the customer with those little extras: a cup of tea while she waited, magazines to read, phone charging during her session, etc.
Loan Officer	You closed your borrower's loan.	ALSO: you got your borrowers a good rate on that loan.	ALSO: you helped your borrowers find the perfect specialized product for their situation and made sure they were up-to-date on the progress of their loan throughout the process.
Retail Sales Clerk	You rang up a purchase.	ALSO: you helped the customers find the right item.	ALSO: you were enthusiastic and helpful throughout their purchase, answering the customers' questions and guiding them to the right item.

Chapter 11

Creative Systems:
The "Clean Windows" Protocols

IN MY LAST YEAR AT COLLEGE, I GOT THE CHANCE TO SING at Disney World.

Okay, not on my own. I'm not that talented. But I was part of an *a cappella* singing group in college, the Georgetown Chimes, and we got invited down to Epcot to perform at an event they were holding.

It was a lot of fun. We rented a Winnebago, drove down from DC to Orlando, stayed in the Fort Wilderness campground, and got a bunch of free tickets to all the parks. Singing at Epcot was an absolute blast.

The day after we performed, we had a free day to visit the Magic Kingdom. So we're walking around, and, as we were wont to do, a few of us broke into song. That's the kind of thing you do when you're in a college *a cappella* group—just start singing at random times and places. Yes, it's completely geeky, and astoundingly annoying. I know. Forgive me, I was young.

Anyway, a few guys started up, the rest of us joined in, and within about 30 seconds we were rollicking through some doo-wop stuff.

It was terrific! People started gathering around us, taking pictures. We finished one song to big applause and launched into another.

And then it stopped. Beefy security guard, really big, polite but firm: "Guys, sorry, I have to stop you."

"Why?"

"Because there's no un-organized singing at Disney."

He was right, of course. We were wrong. We'd been hired to sing a particular song at a particular time and a particular place, not wander around the parks singing whatever we wanted. It didn't matter that people liked it. For Disney to ensure the quality of the experience they give to their visitors, they need to control what their guests see, hear, eat, everything. And we were not, at that moment, under their control. From Disney's perspective, we were a wild card. We might sound terrible, which would reflect badly on them. Or we might launch into ribald drinking songs (very possible, frankly), which would be totally inappropriate for the Disney experience. So they quite correctly stopped us.

That's why Disney World is such a special, magical place, unlike any other theme park in the world.

It's not the rides—you can find more thrilling roller coasters in any run-of-the-mill amusement park.

It's not the food—even though it's kind of fun to walk around gnawing at a drumstick the size of a child's head.

And it's not even Mickey and the gang, who aren't nearly as popular with kids today as the average Nick, Jr. cartoon hero (as someone with a full collection of *Paw Patrol* pups, I know this to be true).

It's not any of those things. Or, rather, it's all of those things, put together. But the common element they all share is simple: Disney exercises precise control over the experience they give their guests to create the magic Disney World is famous for.

I experienced this myself only recently, when my kids were finally old enough to go to Disney World. It was exactly as I remembered it. The employees are always smiling. The park is always spotless. Everything just works. In a million different subtle ways, Disney World is designed to enchant you.

And that's no accident. Think, for example, about how they built Disney World itself. Much of the park is actually on the second floor, built over an underground city that is essentially the "backstage" area where all the performers prepare for their entrances. That's why you never see a guy in a Donald Duck costume hanging out behind a building taking a break, his duck head crooked under his shoulder, smoking a cigarette. Instead, he's downstairs, hiding from all the children.

That kind of thoughtfulness, that attention to detail, that focus on client enchantment, is a Disney trademark. Indeed, one of my favorite stories about client service methodologies is from Bill

Capodagli, who co-authored with Lynn Jackson the great book *The Disney Way*, all about Disney's approach to management and culture.

According to the legend, Bill was at a conference, taking a break sitting by the pool, when a man approached to introduce himself. The man, we'll call him "Jim," told Bill how he ran a midwestern factory, and that his whole business had been changed by *The Disney Way*. Jim explained that after reading the book, he had bought copies for his whole management team, and later for every worker on the line. They'd formed a task force to incorporate *The Disney Way* into their factory, creating a whole policy and procedure guide to ensure the kind of attention to detail for which Disney is famous.

As a final flourish, Jim explained that his task force had come up with a motto that distilled *The Disney Way* for his employees, printing that motto on posters hung throughout the factory, and buttons, hats, and shirts for every employee.

Intrigued, Bill asked, "So what was the motto?"

Proudly, Jim told him: "At our company, we clean the windows as soon as they get dirty."

Let's pause for a moment. Now, as mottos go, "we clean the windows as soon as they get dirty" is not all that great. A little long, a little clunky. But you can appreciate the concept: fix problems as soon as they come up. Don't let things fester. Honestly, I would be pretty happy if every agent and employee in my company made a commitment to fix problems as soon as they came up. I would take that in a second. Not a great motto, but a pretty good standard of practice, all things considered.

But that wasn't good enough for Bill Capodagli. With a rueful smile, he thanked Jim for the kind words, and especially thanked him for buying so many books, but gently explained that the company's motto had missed the point of *The Disney Way*.

Jim was flabbergasted. He missed the point? He'd read the book dozens of times, had to buy an extra copy because he'd marked up his original too many times. How could that be?

So Bill explained that if you wanted to follow the Disney Way, you shouldn't frame your motto as "we clean the windows as soon as they get dirty."

Why?

Because, at Disney, the windows never get dirty.

Mind. Totally. Blown.

Now, I don't know how apocryphal the story is. I've asked Bill about it, and he doesn't remember the particulars, because he speaks to hundreds of audiences and meets thousands of people every year. But he says that the essence of the story is correct, because that is, in fact, the Disney Way.

At Disney, the windows never get dirty.

Think about what that means. You don't wait for the windows to get dirty to clean them. Instead, you set up a schedule to clean them so often that they never actually get dirty.

Now, don't get too literal on me. We're not talking about actual windows, we're using the "Clean Windows" standard as a metaphor for a process you can follow to prevent problems in your business. For example, Bill has told me that Disney used to replace 100,000 light bulbs a year before they ever burned out. They would literally take working light bulbs out of the socket and toss them away. Why? Because that was the only way to ensure that the light bulbs always worked. (These days, of course, Disney uses LED technology, so they probably change them much less frequently).

It's a breathtakingly proactive standard for articulating best practices: don't just fix problems, avoid problems. Create systems that prevent them from happening in the first place. Don't clean the windows when they get dirty, don't let them get dirty.

"The windows never get dirty." That's a motto.

But how do you identify these kinds of best practices? And how do you codify them into systems you can follow? For that, you need what we're going to call "protocols" and "Action Plans."

An Introduction to Protocols

What's a "protocol?" It's just a fancy way of describing a set of procedures that codify the best-practice standard we want to follow. For example, if your best-practice standard is that all light bulbs are working at all times, then the protocol is to schedule their replacement while they're still within their working lifespan. If your standard is always to look your best, then the protocol is to schedule your haircut before you start getting ragged or your roots begin to show.

We can see other examples of these "Clean Windows" protocols in practice at great customer service companies. Consider the

"Starbucks Sweep." Have you ever gotten coffee at a café, gone to the station to get some creamer or sugar, and then been frustrated because the canister or bowl is empty? Or maybe been grossed out because the whole station is filthy? That's not supposed to happen at Starbucks, because the employees are trained to "sweep" that station at a regular time interval, replacing the creamer canisters and refilling the sugar packets. You're never supposed to come across an empty half-and-half canister at a Starbucks, because that's a "dirty window."

We can also see examples of these protocols in things that we do in our own everyday lives. You change the batteries in your smoke detectors every year when you turn back the clocks, rather than waiting for that annoying chirping of a low battery that drives you (and your dog) nuts. You go to the dentist for a cleaning every six months, rather than waiting until you have a toothache. You do a last-minute "sweep" of your hotel room for anything left behind, so you don't lose yet another phone charger still plugged into the wall next to the bed.

Indeed, "Clean Windows" protocols are the basis for all sorts of "preventative maintenance:" it's why we have "Spring Cleaning" every year, why you set your next haircut appointment when you're still at the salon, why you rotate your tires every 10,000 miles or so. It explains those signatures on the inspection forms that you see every time you take an elevator, and the yearly checkups that we do for our fire extinguishers.

But we shouldn't think of the "Clean Windows" protocols as limited to basic maintenance. The idea is simply to set up a standard that eliminates or reduces the possibility of a bad customer experience. Consider the Nordstrom "no questions asked" return policy, which is one of the most successful "Clean Windows" standards in history. Think about how many distracting and damaging customer disputes have been avoided over the years by simply (and generously) setting a protocol that Nordstrom takes returns on anything in any condition. You see a similar protocol at Danny Meyer's Union Square restaurant group, which has a hard and fast rule to take a dish off the bill if the customer complains about it—even if he already ate it! In these cases, the "dirty windows" are customers who are unhappy with what they purchased, and the protocol keeps the windows clean by giving customers their money back, no questions asked. Yes, it might cost money, but it saves time, and drives immense customer satisfaction.

Similarly, geniuses at the Apple Store follow a simple protocol when you bring your phone in for service. Before the genius takes your device from you, she'll ask, "May I touch your iPhone?" That seems silly, right? After all, you brought the phone there because it's not working, and you obviously expect the technician is going to have to touch it to fix it. But Apple found that people are so protective and private about their phones that they had a reflexively negative reaction when technicians touched them. So they created a protocol to relax the customer and keep the window from getting dirty.

And maybe you've heard of the famous Ritz-Carlton protocol for giving directions to guests. If you go to most hotels and ask an employee how you get to "Ballroom C," you might get directions like "Okay, take that escalator over there, make a left at the top, follow that hallway down and then make a right at where the big painting used to be." Not particularly helpful. But at a Ritz-Carlton, if you ask an employee how to get to "Ballroom C," every employee, from the custodian pushing a broom to the president of the company, is taught to stop whatever it is they are doing and take you there. In this case, "dirty windows" are guests wandering around lost in the hotel, and the "take you there myself" protocol is designed to make sure every guest finds her way.

Indeed, the very best "Clean Windows" protocol I ever adopted came from my friend and colleague Bert Waugh, Jr., who founded a legendary brokerage in the Pacific Northwest. And it has nothing whatsoever to do with real estate. Years ago, at a conference, we were all sharing "one great idea" in a workshop. Virtually everyone shared an idea they were using in their business—recruiting tools, coaching programs, things like that. But Bert got up, and for his presentation, told us his great idea: "After I got married, I decided to buy my wife flowers every Friday. And I've been doing it ever since." At that point, he'd been married over 25 years. That's a lot of flowers.

It happened that I was getting married the next year. So I stole his idea, adopting that protocol, and started getting my wife flowers (almost!) every Friday. And it's an amazing thing. Men usually get flowers for their wives on special occasions or when they're in serious trouble. But because I get flowers for my wife every Friday, I generate this weekly burst of affection between us that creates a loving vibe going into the weekend, when we always spend more time together. In other words, those flowers keep my windows clean!

Real Estate Protocols

So how do you apply these types of practices in the real estate industry? If you think about it, you'll find "Clean Windows" protocols in many of the routines you already follow.

For example, here's a specific real estate service protocol I encourage every agent to follow, which goes a long way to maintaining strong agent-client relationships: every Monday, set aside a few hours of "Client Service Time" where you call every single one of your active clients and update them about the market, their transaction, or anything else they might need to know.

Why call your clients every Monday? Too many agents make the mistake of thinking that they only need to call their clients when they have "news." Take, for example, you have a listing, and it's been on the market for a while. In those cases, weeks can go by without any important news—the listing is still on the market, still no showings, still no offers. Indeed, it can be really tough to call clients in those situations, because you feel like you're going to end up in an unpleasant conversation about why nothing is happening.

But that's why you need to call that client every week. After all, no news is still news. And if you don't call, you're just aggravating the situation, because the client takes that as a lack of concern and attention. Which it is.

So you call them every Monday, and you find something to update them about: any new competing listings on the market, any new sales that might impact pricing, any national news about real estate, an update on online property traffic. Basically, fill them in on anything you can think of. And also take the opportunity while you're on the phone to do some basic maintenance of the listing: ask them whether the sign is still up, and how well they're maintaining the condition of the home. And while you're at it, pull up the listing on your laptop to check that it's showing up in searches and that the pictures are seasonally appropriate.

Similarly, you call all your buyers every Monday. You find out if they went to any open houses over the weekend, do a quick search to see if anything new has hit the market, and maybe even set your showing schedule with them for the week.

And you call every one of your clients who are in contract, to update them on the progress toward closing. Even if you have nothing to report, you let them know that you're still working on it. At the very least, that discipline to call all your clients on Monday will force you to get your own updates from the loan officers, attorneys, escrow agency, or whoever else is holding the deal up.

That Monday client call is really important in keeping your windows clean. For one thing, your clients feel the reassurance of knowing that they're going to talk to you at least every week, so they'll never complain about a lack of communication. For another, the Monday call takes the pressure off the rest of the week. If your clients know that you're going to talk every Monday, they're less likely to pepper you with non-urgent calls during the week, and especially on the weekend. They'll just wait until your Monday talk.

Most importantly, though, the Monday call sets an expectation you can meet. The biggest mistake agents make is when they tell a client, "I'm always available to you." That's a terrible thing to say, because it sets an unreasonable expectation that you're never going to be able to live up to. And it's not true! Sometimes, you're not available to that client—you're with another client, or with your kids, or sleeping. All you're doing is setting yourself up for failure. Don't do that. Set reasonable expectations for your clients, and you'll have a better experience working with them and them with you.

The Monday "Client Service Time" is just one example of protocols that I know agents have incorporated into their business. Here are some others:

- Always take professional photos for every listing, regardless of price point, so that every listing looks beautifully-marketed. Either learn professional photography or hire someone to do it for you.

- Always write property descriptions in word processors that have spell-checking, so that you never have goofy abbreviations or misspellings in your listings.

- Always do a thorough CMA on a listing that you're making an offer on for your buyers, so you can ensure they're fully informed about current market conditions.

- Always complete a "red flag" compliance search when you take a listing, checking for liens on the property, getting accurate tax information, and identifying any outstanding departmental violations, so that you're never surprised later on in the transaction.

- Never meet someone you don't know at a house for sale, which is unprofessional and dangerous.

- Google every client before your first appointment to gather information about her or look for personal connections that might help generate rapport.

- Always keeps three sets of onboarding documents in your trunk, so that you're never caught unprepared for a spontaneous seller or buyer appointment.

These are just examples. The point is, think creatively about bright-line rules that you could set for your business that will keep those windows clean.

Here are some guidelines you can follow:

First, identify the best practices you want to follow. Your protocols should articulate the ideal ways of doing things in your business, following the most ambitious standards you can manage. Guiding a guest to Ballroom C is a higher level of care than giving that guest directions. Think hard about what you could be doing better for your clients, and turn those practices into protocols.

Second, keep things as simple as possible. The best protocols are "bright line" rules that are easy to understand and follow. The "no questions asked" return policy. "Can I touch your device?" You don't have to think about it, you don't have to make hard decisions about how to apply it, you just have to do it.

Third, try to automate everything you can. The most effective protocols become internalized routines—habits that we follow automatically and raise our level of performance almost unconsciously. If you work at Starbucks, you develop an internal clock that tells you it's time to go do the "sweep." Even better, find ways to *literally* automate your protocol so that you don't actually have to do anything to implement it.

Finally, you need to find a way to codify all these protocols into a system you can follow consistently. And for that, you need what we'll call an "Action Plan."

Chapter 12

Executing Well:
The "No Brown M&Ms" Action Plans

"No brown M&Ms!"

When the rock band Van Halen went on the road in the 1970s, they made outrageous demands on their concert promoters. They wanted all the usual perks of rock star travel, including luxurious suites, chauffeured limos, and lavish buffets.

They also had a very specific, and slightly quirky, demand: in their dressing room, they wanted a bowl of M&Ms. But not just any M&Ms—they wanted yellow M&Ms, red M&Ms, orange M&Ms, green M&Ms, and blue M&Ms.

But no brown M&Ms. Never any brown M&Ms. The contract rider literally said: "M&Ms (*WARNING: ABSOLUTELY NO BROWN ONES*)."

Really. That's what the band required: a bowl of M&Ms, with all the brown ones removed. If they saw brown M&Ms in that bowl, they had the right to cancel the contract. Which is crazy, of course. I mean, I hate to break this to you, but M&Ms all taste the same!

The story became a famous example of rock star excess, and cultural shorthand for "prima donna behavior." If one of your friends acts like a diva, or makes outrageous and pointless demands, you joke that she wants you to take out the brown M&Ms.

It's a totally true story. Ironically, though, it had nothing to do with prima donna frivolity. Quite the opposite—it's an amazing example of creating a standard to ensure attention to best practices.

Years later, lead singer David Lee Roth explained the purpose of the Brown M&M Rider. According to Roth, Van Halen was constantly touring throughout the country, with concerts one after another.

They might be in Philadelphia one night, New York the next night, then on to Boston. And they had an elaborate stage show with moving platforms, massive speakers, intricate lighting, the whole bit. So the band was concerned that, with the pace of the tour, and the complexity of the equipment, the promoters might not be able to set up the staging correctly. Not only might that ruin the show, but it could create a safety hazard for the band or its fans.

To protect against inattentive promoters, Van Halen put together a set of elaborate contract terms that specified every single intricate detail of the staging requirements—everything from the amperage required for outlets to the weight tolerances necessary for flooring.

And on top of everything else? Absolutely no brown M&Ms. But not because the band cared about the flavor of the candies. Rather, the rider was a simple but effective way of testing the promoter's attention to detail. The band often pulled into the stadium with little time for a full inspection. They might not have time to test the electrical wiring, or the staging, or any of the other major systems.

But they could check a bowl of M&Ms. If Roth walked into the dressing room and saw that the bowl had been picked clean of brown M&Ms, he felt confident that the promoters were paying attention to the rider. If they took the time to pick out those M&Ms, they likely also took the time to follow the lighting instructions.

If Roth saw brown M&Ms, though, all hell would break loose. He'd tear up the dressing room, throw a fit, and insist on a complete inspection of the facilities, even if it delayed the show. In other words, the M&M bowl was like the canary in the coal mine, signaling whether the facility was safe.

So the Brown M&M Rider is not, in fact, an example of prima donna behavior. Rather, it's an example of the single most effective way of ensuring great execution: an Action Plan

The ~~Checklist~~ Action Plan

What's an "Action Plan?" Well, the Action Plan is the key to the whole system, a codification of all your protocols into a set of action steps, a list that you can...you know...check off...uh...when you complete them.

Okay, okay, I admit, it's just a checklist.

A simple checklist.

A mundane checklist.

A boring old checklist.

A beautiful, elegant, life-saving checklist.

Hear me out. Checklists are wonderful things. I know they might sometimes seem silly, almost prosaic, and you're probably wondering why you paid for, or bothered to steal, this book for banal advice like this.

But hear me out—checklists save lives. Like the lives of rock stars who want a simple way to check to make sure that their stage is safe.

Or the lives of surgical patients. In his wonderful book *The Checklist Manifesto*, surgeon Atul Gawande details how the World Health Organization developed what's called the "Surgical Safety Checklist" in an exhaustive effort to reduce errors that often result in post-operative infections. You'd think that doctors wouldn't need something as mundane as a checklist to perform a successful surgery. Indeed, if you read the "Surgical Safety Checklist," you would almost laugh at the banality of some of the items:

- *Has the patient confirmed his/her identity, site, procedure, and consent?*

- *Is the site marked?*

- *Confirm all team members have introduced themselves by name and role.*

Really? You're a doctor, and you're about to start an operation, and you have to introduce yourself to everyone else? You have to mark the area for the surgery? Seems crazy, right?

Except that it's not. The point of the Surgical Safety Checklist is that doctors are human, and they make mistakes. And hospitals are often large, complicated bureaucratic organizations that make mistakes, too.

What kinds of mistakes? Well, the reason the checklist requires that the patient confirm his identity is that doctors have occasionally performed surgery on the wrong patient. Just a slight mix-up! And the checklist also requires the surgeon to confirm that the site of the procedure is marked, so that, say, she amputates the correct leg. Literally, surgeons doing prep work will take a magic marker and write "NOT THIS LEG!" on the other leg.

And that bit about everyone introducing themselves? That's included so that, later on, if the operation is going sideways and things are getting hectic, the surgeon knows who everyone is and the role they're playing in the operation.

In other words, every part of the checklist has a purpose. And it works. According to one study published in the *New England Journal of Medicine* that reviewed the results in eight pilot hospitals, the checklist reduced the rate of deaths and surgical complications by more than a third. The rate of major inpatient complications fell by 37%, and the rate of inpatient death following major operations fell by 47%.

That is, checklists save lives.

Indeed, your own life has probably been saved by a checklist, even if you don't know it. After all, you've flown on a plane, right? What do you think that pilots use to ensure a safe takeoff and landing? They use a checklist. Like, when pilot Chesley "Sully" Sullenberger landed a disabled plane on the Hudson River without a single fatality in 2009, he and his co-pilot expressed their appreciation for the exhaustive flight checklists that the National Transportation Safety Board has prepared for every possible in-flight emergency.

And you've certainly been inside a skyscraper built through the use of painstakingly-prepared blueprints that are themselves a series of checklists designed to make sure that the building doesn't fall down around your head.

Everyone uses checklists. You ever watch one of the many variations of the television show *Law & Order*, when the detectives come across a dead body and start their investigation? What's the first thing that they do? They "start a canvass," which is a rigorous building-by-building, door-by-door search of the entire neighborhood to look for witnesses. Then they check credit card statements and interview family members, and all the rest of that fun stuff. You know what they're following? An investigative checklist.

So let's have a little respect for checklists, shall we? Let's acknowledge that if doctors can use them during surgery, and pilots can use them on flights, and architects can use them building skyscrapers, and detectives can use them for investigations, and even rock stars can use them when making sure their shows are safe, then you can use them when you're managing your clients.

Here's an example. Let's say that you just took a listing, and you bring the paperwork back to the office. Now, you have to get that listing on the market. So what are some of the things you might need to do?

✓ Get photos taken.

✓ Write a property description.

✓ Enter the data into the MLS grid.

✓ Order a sign.

✓ Order a lockbox.

✓ Write up showing instructions.

✓ Check the property taxes.

✓ Check for recorded building code violations.

✓ Prepare online marketing like an email blast.

✓ Prepare direct mail mailing.

You probably do most of those things when you take a listing, right? So the point of the checklist isn't to give you some new work to do, it's just to identify the best practices, codify them, and then give you a way to track the work that you're already supposed to be doing.

Let's say, for example, that you tried to do all these things without a checklist. That's certainly possible. After all, you've taken a lot of listings before, and you know the routine like the back of your hand. So you wing it.

In most cases, that's no problem: you manage to get everything done. Except this one time you got a little distracted when you got back to the office. You got most of the tasks completed, but you forgot to fill out the sign order, and so the sign didn't go up. A day passes, a few more days, a week. You don't know the sign didn't go up, because you haven't been by the house since it hit the market.

So a week later, you get a call from your seller: "Where is my sign?"

Guess what? Your windows are filthy.

And that's why you use a checklist, because you will find no better way to ensure that you complete every single detail for getting that listing on the market.

Of course, it's not just for taking a listing. You need checklists for when you take a buyer out for the first time, when you present an offer, when you have to guide the client from contract to closing, and every other part of managing your client's experience. Anytime you can identify a set of "Clean Windows" best practices that you want to follow the same way, the right way, every time, you need a checklist.

Even better, your checklists can get sophisticated, and go beyond the simple ministerial tasks that you need to complete to take a listing or intake a buyer. Maybe, for example, your new listing checklist includes the steps you have to follow to make a listing video or create a coffee-table book. Maybe you create checklists of everything you need to do on your Monday Client Service calls.

Indeed, it's not just about the transactional aspect of your work. Create checklists for your client development work, setting out a series of tasks you have to complete each week to contact your past clients. Or create a checklist that you'll follow to prepare for every listing presentation or buyer presentation. In other words, any time you have a set of tasks that you want to complete the right way every time, you should codify them in a checklist.

Here's an example. Every three months, I put together a quarterly market report for our clients to review current market conditions. It's a lot of work. I have to pull all the data from the MLS, organize it, analyze it, and then write up a series of market reports for each of the counties that we cover. Once that's done, I send it to my marketing people so that they can create all the graphs and tables and lay out the reports in a pretty design. And then when they're finished, it's back to me for a painstaking proofing process to ensure that we don't make any mistakes. The whole process is extremely complicated and arduous, and we have to do it under intense time pressure to get the report out while the information is still fresh. It's the worst week of my quarter, every quarter.

So how do we do it? We follow a checklist that sets out every task necessary to complete the report. That checklist is essential for making sure we follow the best practices every single time. For example, I always double-check the data for inaccuracies that would throw off our calculations, because agents sometimes make mistakes when they enter their listings. They might put in a $500,000 listing as a $5,000,000 listing, which throws off the listing price retention rate: i.e., when that listing sells for $490,000, it should only count as a 2% price reduction, not a 90% reduction. But if I wasn't using a checklist, I might forget to do that double-check, and end up with an inaccurate report.

But it's not just about making the report better. The checklist makes the report easier for me to complete. I don't have to think about all the steps I need to take to get the report done. I don't have to "reinvent the wheel" every quarter. I just go through the tasks on the checklist, which is a lot easier than keeping it all in my head.

This is the Job!

Listen, I know what you're probably thinking, because I've heard it all from my own agents:

I don't need a checklist to tell me how to do my job.

I already know how to do this.

You're treating me like a child!

Oh, great, another form I have to fill out!

I get it. I really do. Checklists seem like such a jejune way of ensuring high-level execution of your "Clean Windows" protocols. Even though surgeons and pilots and architects and detectives all use them, they still carry a stigma of simple-mindedness.

That's why I call them "Action Plans." That sounds better, right? Action Plan! It's got the word "action" in it and everything, and "action" is a super-cool word. And "plan," another good word! So much more exciting than a mere "checklist."

Indeed, let's review some of the real benefits you get from using these ~~checklists~~ Action Plans in your business:

First, the Action Plan creates an automatic consistency and attention to detail in your client service. Why do people go to Starbucks, or McDonald's, or Google? Because they love consistency. If you want to do the same thing the same way every time, and you should, then you need to follow a plan that sets out every task you have to complete.

Second, the Action Plan takes your mind off the mundane details of your work, freeing you to be creative. Anytime you can work from a checklist rather than out of your head, you free up the RAM in your brain to work on something else. Most of the items on your Action Plan are ministerial, so there's no reason for you to "wing it" every time you have to take care of your clients. You don't need to be "creative" in the way you order the sign—you either order it or you don't. Using the checklist clears out the little stuff and frees up brain space to get creative about the big stuff.

Third, the Action Plans give you a great way to track your progress. A good Plan is like a "to do" list for that particular project, so you get that same feeling of satisfaction and accomplishment of a "job well done" as you move through the list.

Fourth, the Action Plans give you a way to articulate your best practices. You can literally sit down and identify all the "Clean Windows" protocols that you want to employ in your business, and just write them down into a Plan that will ensure that you do them rigorously for all your clients.

Finally, the Action Plan becomes a physical manifestation of your commitment to providing your clients with a great service experience. My agents can literally take the plans out of their folders and show them to their prospective clients at listing and buyer consultations as a way of demonstrating the attention to detail that the clients can expect of them. Everyone says that they provide "great service" to their clients, but very few agents can actually demonstrate that commitment with a visual Showpiece.

The best Action Plans are the ones you create for yourself, because every agent has their own approach to the business. But if you want to see some examples of the plans that we've created for our agents, go to www.joerand.com and look for the agent resources we have available.

Now, I recognize that agents sometimes see these Action Plans as additional work they need to complete. Even worse, a checklist is yet another form that agents have to fill out when they're working with a client. "Don't we have enough forms?"—that's a question I get a lot.

But here's the thing: this is the job. You can't be a real estate agent and complain about forms. It's like becoming a dentist and then complaining about teeth—that's the job!

So try it out. Sit down and write out a list of the best practices you want to follow in different aspects of your business: taking a listing, showing a house, managing a transaction, canvassing a neighborhood. Then codify those best practices in an Action Plan. Then follow that plan every time. It'll make your job easier.

And if it makes your job easier, it'll help you get better at it.

Chapter 13

The Ten Elements of Great Client Experiences

A FEW YEARS AGO, I USED TO GO TO A LOCAL BAKERY AND coffeehouse called Columbus Bakery on 83rd Street, around the corner from where I lived in Manhattan. They had good coffee, and it was a convenient stop on the way to my parking garage.

But I was always annoyed by the lines. Basically, they had one line for everyone, whether you were getting a dozen bagels, selecting muffins, or just picking up (as I usually was) a simple cup of coffee. I'd invariably find myself behind someone who was asking a million questions about, say, the fruit tarts. Frustrating, but I always try to patronize local businesses. Also, it was closer than walking an extra block to the Starbucks, and I'm very, very lazy.

One morning, I go to Columbus Bakery for a breakfast meeting with a colleague. We wait on the long line and order a coffee for me and a muffin and iced tea for him. I pay, get my receipt, and go to yet another line to pick up our stuff.

That's when the problems start. I show the receipt to the woman behind the counter, and she gets me the iced tea and the muffin, then turns away. I stop her and ask for the coffee, and she looks again at the receipt.

"You didn't buy a coffee."

I look at the receipt. She's right. There's no coffee on it.

"Oh, sorry, I guess she didn't hear me. I also need a large coffee."

Now, think about how this could have played out. The barista could have just gotten me a cup of coffee, charged me for it right there, and brought the money to the cashier. Or she could have gotten me a coffee on the house, apologizing for the cashier getting the order wrong. It's just a cup of coffee. And it was pretty obvious that I meant to order it—it's not like my colleague and I were going to split an iced tea.

Instead, here's what she says:

"You need to go back in line."

I look over, there are 10 more people on the line. I already went through the line. I didn't like it so much the first time. I have no interest in a second turn. This is not a good option.

So I plead for a little consideration. I say:

"Listen, can't you just get me a cup of coffee? I'm happy to pay for it. I really did order it."

And she says:

"That's not my problem."

That's not my problem. The kind of thing you expect to hear at the DMV, from a civil servant with job protection. Not at, you know, an actual business that needs to make people happy in order to earn a profit. So now I am annoyed:

"That's not your problem? Whose problem is it, then? Your manager? Can I talk to him or her?"

Yes, I go there. I throw down the "can I talk to the manager?" card. I'm not proud of this. It was, after all, just a cup of coffee. But it's not about the coffee. It's not about getting back in that horrible line. Now, it's about "that's not my problem."

Ultimately, though, the "call the manager" gambit works. The last thing this woman wants is to have to keep dealing with me, because, in her eyes, I am a terribly annoying person (many people would agree with her). So she rolls her eyes, grabs a cup, fills it with coffee, and hands it to me. And when I try to give her some money, she refuses it, saying, "Just take it."

So let's think about how this played out. She wasted a lot of time, annoyed a customer, got riled up, and then to top it all off gave away a free cup of coffee anyway. Not her best work.

The next day, I started walking the extra block to Starbucks.

Columbus Bakery went out of business a few months later.

Now, they didn't go out of business because they lost out on selling me a cup of coffee every morning. But my experience was probably a signal of bigger problems in employee morale, training, culture, you name it. Sometimes, a line out the door is a good sign that you have a popular product. Other times, a line out the door is a terrible sign that you have a really bad system of selling your product.

Sometimes, it's a sign that you're not very good at your job.

Be Great at Your Job

Too many people don't want to be great at their jobs. It's not like they wake up in the morning, stretch, and then joyfully exclaim, "I'm going to do a really crappy job today." It's more like they just don't care too much about the work they do.

Maybe they don't like their job, so they don't put energy into doing it well.

Maybe they like their job, but they're not well-trained, so they don't have the knowledge or skills to do it well.

Or maybe the job is just really, really hard, and it's difficult to be great at it.

Take, for example, my Columbus Bakery barista. I have no idea why she would have shown such contempt for a customer with a relatively reasonable request. Maybe she never got decent training at customer service. Maybe she wasn't well-managed. Maybe she just didn't care enough to try to do a good job. Heck, maybe she was a wonderful barista, but was having a rough day. But whatever the reason, at least that particular day, she was bad at her job.

You don't have that luxury. You're not getting a salary. You're not in a union. You're not a worker drone that no one notices. You're an entrepreneur, basically a small business owner, which means that if you want to be successful, you need to be great at your job.

And if you want to be great at your job, you have to recognize a fundamental truth about great service: it's not about "service" at all.

It's not about you.

It's about them.

It's not about your "service," it's about their "experience."

That is, we shouldn't try to define "great service" from the perspective of the provider, but from the perspective of the recipient. It's not what you do, it's what they feel. It's almost like what Justice Potter Stewart once famously said about defining pornography: "I know it when I see it."

Talking about "service" is being agent-oriented: it focuses on you, and what you do. What we need to do is think about the clients, and the experience they want and need.

For example, let's say that I walk into a men's clothing store at the mall to waste some time while my wife is shopping. A clerk comes up and I shoo-shoo her away because I don't want to be annoyed by someone trying to sell me something. I don't need "help." I'm just looking. I just want the clerk to leave me alone to walk around on my own.

A week later, I go into the same store, except this time I'm in a rush because I spilled coffee on my tie and I need a new one for a big meeting. This time, the clerk comes up to help me, and I'm grateful. She guides me to the ties, helps me pick one out, rings me up.

It's the same clerk, providing the same exact service, but two completely different experiences. Why? Not because the clerk did anything differently, but because my needs changed.

In other words, "great service" is in the eye of the beholder, the recipient, the person receiving the service.

So if we really want to be great at our jobs, we have to focus not on ourselves, and the service we provide, but on the experiences we give our clients.

But how do we ensure that we provide great experiences? For years, I've talked to audiences about client experiences, and heard hundreds of memorable stories, both good and bad. And I've studied great "customer service" companies in all industries, to try to learn how they create the experiences for which they're famous. What I've discovered is that great service experiences usually have certain characteristics in common, qualities that come up again and again in the stories I hear from audiences and the research I've done.

Luckily, there are exactly 10 of them, which makes for a nice round number:

1. **Detail:** Exercising focused attention on the "little things" to get them right.

2. **Consistency:** Providing the same quality experience every time in every situation.

3. **Enthusiasm:** Exhibiting a passion for providing outstanding client care.

4. **Expertise:** Possessing comprehensive product knowledge and well-developed service skills.

5. **Connection:** Forging an authentic personal link with a client.

6. **Communication:** Keeping the client up-to-date and fully informed throughout the transaction.

7. **Generosity:** Putting the clients' needs first, giving them the benefit of the doubt and erring to their benefit.

8. **Empowerment:** Giving all representatives the authority to make decisions in the best interests of the client.

9. **Resilience:** Treating mistakes as opportunities to go "above and beyond" and create memorable experiences.

10. **Delight:** Surprising the client with an unexpected sense of enchantment.

Let's go over each of these characteristics, how they've been articulated by some of these great companies, and the challenges to, and opportunities for, applying them in real estate.

1. Detail. Little things are important. Clean bathrooms at the diner. A smile at the register. New magazines in the waiting room. That's why attention to detail is such an important part of a great client service experience, because every single interaction, no matter how small, can make a big impression. Disney is legendary for this kind of attention to detail, which you know if you've ever visited one of their theme parks. When he was designing his first park, Walt Disney famously took a walk while eating a hot dog, so he could calculate how many steps someone would take before finishing and throwing away the wrapper, which is why Disney park trash cans are all about 30 feet from one another. If you finish that hot dog and can't find a trash can, you probably wolfed it down. Take your time!

That sort of attention to detail is a real challenge in real estate, because of the sheer complexity of a transaction that has so many different moving parts assembled by an array of unrelated professionals. You might do a flawless job staging and marketing the home, presenting and negotiating offers, and then getting your client into contract, only to have the client go through a hellish experience when the escrow company drops the ball on the title work. You not only have to exercise control over your own work but find a way to facilitate everyone else's.

But remember that you do control your own work, and you need to apply that same level of attention to everything you do for your clients. Make sure the sign goes up in the right place. Check that the photos are in the correct order. Correct the detailing of the home every time you visit. People notice that attention to detail, and it makes a difference.

2. Consistency. The same experience every single time. Every. Single. Time. Great businesses find ways to ensure that kind of consistency: McDonald's, Lowe's, Costco, Starbucks, Dunkin' Donuts. Think of the challenge of maintaining consistency not just in your own business, but for myriad locations spread throughout the country. And yet they do it. You go to McDonald's, anywhere in the country—anywhere in the world!—and the fries all taste the same. You go into a Costco, and it looks like a Costco. A Frappuccino is a Frappuccino. That's consistency.

From the perspective of a real estate broker, consistency is almost impossible to achieve. I've got over 1,000 real estate agents at my company, and I have frustratingly little control over what they do on a day-to-day basis. Unlike the manager at a McDonald's, or at a Costco, I can't watch over them when they're making presentations in someone's living room or taking buyers out in their cars. The best I can do is provide training that guides agents in making the right decisions, system support to make their jobs easier, and do as much as I can to provide great services directly to the client where possible. But even then, if a client walks into one office and meets with Agent A, and then another client walks into a different office and meets with Agent B, those two clients might have completely divergent experiences, even though both agents have access to the same tools, systems, and resources. So from a broker's perspective, consistency is really tough.

And it's not much easier for you as an agent. While you have the power to be consistent in your own actions, doing the same thing the same way every time, you can't always account for how your clients' expectations will change -- the way that I wanted something different when I walked into that clothing store the second time.

Even worse, I don't think the industry fully appreciates and prepares for how real estate agents have to build the skills and processes to serve two completely separate types of clients: buyers and sellers. We lump them all together as "clients," but, in reality, they require two completely different experiences. Some of the basics are the same—managing the transaction, communicating, problem-solving. But for sellers, you need skills in marketing, pricing, and staging. For buyers, you need to know how to read a client, help them search for a home, and qualify them. Those are two completely different service dynamics.

It's like if McDonald's sold hamburgers and also did your taxes. It's tough to do both of those things well every time. But you have to if you want to provide outstanding client experiences.

3. Enthusiasm. If you want to provide a great experience, you have to evince a passion for your work that is almost palpable. It's not always easy. Take air travel, for instance. That's a really tough sector for providing good experiences, simply because flying is stressful, wearying, time-consuming, and subject to all sorts of frustrating delays. In most surveys of customer service, airlines (along with cable companies) usually finish near the bottom. Except for Southwest Airlines, which somehow manages to create good customer experiences even in this most challenging of environments. Why? Lots of reasons, but I can't help but think that the unique enthusiasm that Southwest crew members bring to their jobs is the most important. They sing. They tell jokes. They engage. They seem to like their jobs and their company, and that kind of enthusiasm is infectious.

ENTHUSIASM

This is one area where real estate agents can excel. You control your attitude, so if you want to be enthusiastic about your job, you can be. No one else will do it for you, and one no else can screw it up for you. It's all up to you. And, in fact, I generally think that agents do bring enthusiasm and passion to their work. After all, the part of the job most of them enjoy the most is working with buyers and sellers, at least compared to the agonies of lead generation. So it's almost a relief when they get to take out a buyer.

Sadly, though, enthusiasm is one of those qualities that is necessary but not sufficient. We've all had waiters who come across like gangbusters when we first sit down: "I'm Bobby, I'm going to be your server today, so happy to have you with us!" Big smile! Fun demeanor! But an hour later, when you still haven't gotten your entrees, and he never refilled the bread basket, and he was wrong when he told you the soup didn't have any gluten, and now you're breaking out in hives – that's when you realize that enthusiasm without expertise is a broken promise.

4. Expertise. You have to know your stuff and possess the skills to use your knowledge effectively. We've all had the sublime experience of being in the care of a really knowledgeable service professional: the electrician who finds the flaw in your wiring, the doctor who correctly diagnoses your illness, the lawyer who knows exactly how to draft your agreement. And we've all had the miserable experience of finding out that we put our faith in people who didn't know what they were talking about.

Apple really stands out here, not just for the expertise they demonstrate in their manufacturing, but in what they've accomplished in the Apple Store. Traditionally, buying electronics has always been a hassle, and getting your equipment repaired, virtually impossible. You might as well take that broken laptop and throw it in the river. That changed with the Apple Store, where enthusiastic "Geniuses" will figure out what's wrong and how you can fix it. And they know their stuff. I've personally been there 15 or 20 times with problems, and I've never stumped them yet. It's not always cheap, but I never feel like they're at a loss on how to help me.

It's not easy for real estate agents to develop that level of expertise. Not only do you have to master an immensely complicated transactional environment, but you need to develop a vast array of skills: counseling, problem-solving, marketing, presenting, negotiating, communicating, and so on. That's what makes the typical "new agent training program" that starts with cold calling and ends with even more cold calling such an abomination.

Even harder, you have to stay on top of an ever-changing inventory at escalating price levels. I remember going to a car dealership and asking a question about whether the sedan or the SUV was longer, and waiting while the car salesperson had to look it up. He had five vehicle models in stock, just five, and they were the same five last year and the year before that, and he still had to look up to find out how long they were. How productive could you be if you only had to keep track of five houses in inventory?

That's what makes maintaining expertise in real estate so difficult. What we're selling changes every day. Even the geniuses at Apple only have to service their own products—they don't need to know how to fix a Samsung phone.

5. Connection. A few years ago, I was lucky enough to stay at a Four Seasons Hotel in Hawaii (even luckier, someone else was paying). My wife and I checked in late at night and went to breakfast the next morning. As I approached the restaurant hostess, she looked at us and said, "Welcome, Mr. and Ms. Rand."

She knew who we were. Just to be clear, we had not made a reservation for breakfast, we weren't wearing name tags, and we were far from the only guests at the hotel. But they knew who were. And after a long day of traveling and a short jet-lagged night of sleep, it was a welcome personal touch.

And it was a neat trick. Such a simple thing, knowing someone's name. But that kind of personal connection is a key to great customer experience. Their knowing my name sent me a message that I was valued, that I was important to them. And that set the tone for the entire stay.

In the real estate business, that kind of personal touch is vital. We're supposed to be fiduciary representatives of people who are making one of the most important financial decisions possible, and guiding them through a process that most of them will only experience a few times in their lives. We need their trust, their confidence, their faith—which is only possible if we can make a personal connection to them.

The challenge, of course, is that we often have to overcome the skepticism and suspicion that people bring to interactions with "salespeople," particularly when we're meeting potential clients for the first time. And it doesn't help if we launch into that rote one-size-fits-all "presentation" that we were taught when we first got our license. That's why it's so important to build rapport with your clients through the simple process of asking them questions and showing an authentic interest in their answers. You need that personal touch to set the tone for the rest of your relationship, and you can't be "personal" if you're delivering a "one size fits all" script that you give all your potential clients.

6. Communication. A great client experience requires keeping the client informed at every step of the transaction. Amazon is one of the great service companies of our age, for example, in part because of how well it communicates with its customers. If you buy something from Amazon, you can track its progress all the way through the system, and even get alerts every time it passes through a checkpoint: it's been ordered, it's been packaged, it's been shipped, it's out for delivery, it was delivered, it didn't fit, it was returned, etc.

COMMUNICATION

This should be easy for real estate agents. After all, we've never had so many different ways to connect with our clients: call, email, text, social media, or even, you know, seeing them in person. If anything, with the technology available to us today, we should be *over-communicating.*

But here's the challenge: it's never been easier to communicate, and we've never communicated worse. All of us. Not just agents. Everyone. It's almost like we have too many ways to reach one another that we generate too much content to process effectively.

That's why, in my experience, 90% of the bad client reviews we see in the real estate industry blame a lack of communication. How can that be? Most of the time, it's just a disconnect between client and agent expectations. The client thought that she would hear from the agent more regularly, and the agent only reached out when she had news. You need to make sure you set those expectations with your clients, that you know how often they want to hear from you, and how.

Other times, though, a lack of communication is a signal of a bigger problem: a bad relationship that got worse when the agent started avoiding calling the client out of a reluctance to get into yet another argument. It's like a marriage—when a couple has problems, their communication suffers. So you need to identify when your relationship with your client is deteriorating, and fight that urge to avoid calling them. Indeed, it's even more important to reach out when the relationship is imperiled. Don't let your reluctance to talk to an unhappy client induce you into making things worse by ignoring them.

7. Generosity. Great companies put clients and their needs first. They design their systems to put the clients' interests front and center, and often err on the side of the clients in any disputes or conflicts. Nordstrom has become legendary for its "no questions asked" returns policy, which, famously, has included them taking back merchandise that they don't even sell! Why would they do such a thing? Goodwill is part of it, as is their general customer-centrism, but so is the fact that every time I've returned something at Nordstrom to get a refund, I've spent even more money buying something else. In other words, the policy is not just good for the customer, it's good business.

You see this kind of generosity in great organizations. Restaurants that will take a mostly-eaten entrée off the check if you say it wasn't cooked properly. Hotels that will waive the cancellation fees when you tell them that you're too sick to travel. Doctors who do follow-up consultations without putting them on the books when you still haven't recovered. They don't bicker, they don't haggle, they just take your word for it. Does this mean that they sometimes get taken advantage of by swindlers who will lie about their situation? Of course. But that's the cost of doing business. They'll still err on the side of trusting their clients or patients.

We have a real challenge trying to be this big-hearted in real estate. Unlike some of these famously generous companies, we provide relatively expensive services in situations where clients are often unhappy about situations well beyond our control and might take it out on us, and out of our pocket, if we allowed for "refunds." Like, you might earn thousands of dollars getting a home into contract, provide a great client service experience, and then get tarred with a broad unhappy brush when the title company messes things up at the end. It might be ruinous if you routinely refunded that compensation for unhappy clients.

GENEROSITY

So I'm not going to get too self-righteous about how real estate companies should offer "money back guarantees." After all, you don't often see this kind of generosity in high-ticket items: try bringing back your car after driving it for a week. Go ask for your money back after an expensive, and bad, Broadway show. Tell the doctor you're not paying for the facelift, since you still look old. It's a lot easier to write off a $40 entrée that took 10 minutes to prepare than a $25,000 fee that required six months of work.

That said, we've started to see some companies across the country test out this sort of thing—a "pay what you want" approach that "suggests" a fee to their clients and trusts that they will pay a reasonable amount for a good service provided. But that's a tough program to pull off, especially when brokerages are comprised of independent contractors who might not be willing to entrust their livelihood to the better angels of every single client. And if you've worked in this business long enough, you know that some clients simply cannot be satisfied no matter what you do, and they are the ones who will "return" their fully eaten salmon every time.

Arguably, we already provide for a level of "generosity" by charging our fees only when the transaction is complete. We don't get paid for the hours we spend working with clients who ultimately choose not to buy or sell—we just swallow it. Similarly, we might spend thousands of dollars and dozens (or hundreds!) of hours on a real estate deal, only to make nothing when it falls apart at the last minute through no fault of our own. We don't turn around and send a bill for our hourly rate.

But "generosity" doesn't just mean a "no questions asked" refund policy. It incorporates a general sense of putting the client first. For example, I can tell how well a company values its clients just by pulling into the parking lot and checking out whether they have allotted parking spaces to clients or visitors. Too many companies are filled with employees who are what I call "near parkers," who take the best spaces in the lot and leave nothing for the customers who actually pay their salaries. Go to most malls at 9:30 in the morning and you'll see that the first 20 spaces in every row are already taken and will remain taken for another eight hours or so until the end of the first shift. That's not a generous, client-driven approach. It's a small thing, but meaningful.

8. Empowerment. Rules are important. Professional organizations rely on well-developed policies and procedures to ensure compliance with everything from ethics to regulations to internal service standards.

EMPOWERMENT

But you have to know when to break the rules, too. That's why great client experience organizations empower their front-line personnel, the people who actually work with clients every day in the field, with the authority to make exceptions to standard operating procedure in the interest of the higher cause of satisfying an important client need. After all, what's worse than hearing something like, "Sir, I can't do that, it's a company policy"?

I recently had an experience like that with the restaurant chain Dave & Buster's. I had won a $50 gift certificate at a charity auction about six months earlier and took the kids to go to D&B's to get some lunch and play some games. But when they looked at the certificate, they realized it had expired about a month earlier.

Now, fair's fair. The gift certificate had a valid expiration date on it, and it was my fault that I didn't use it in time. I wouldn't have blamed them for refusing to honor it, although, I confess, I would have been a bit annoyed. But the staffer didn't even blink at it. Perhaps she looked over and realized it was lunchtime, I had two kids with me, and I was likely to spend a whole lot more than $50 over the next few hours. Or maybe she took pity on a hapless dad. Either way, she barely thought about it before smiling and agreeing to honor the certificate. And then I went and spent lots more money. Lots. More. Money. But it was fine, because at the end my kids were able to turn in their fistfuls of tickets to get a plastic comb!

Unfortunately, real estate agents work in a highly-regulated environment in which "the rules" often refer to procedures set up to protect them from liability, legal trouble, or ethics problems. So it's not always quite as easy to compromise on a policy. In our company, for example, agents do not get paid unless their disclosures are all completed. That's a hard-and-fast policy that has (knock on wood) kept us free from regulator problems for almost 20 years. And we don't make exceptions to it lightly, because we know that holding back those checks is the best way to ensure crucial regulatory compliance.

But, in cases where our policies don't implicate legal or regulatory issues but are just internal controls, I hope and expect that my agents know when to relax the rules in service of a client's needs. For example, we have standards for commission rates, terms of agreements, and things like that, but give agents the flexibility to make exceptions in situations where they think it's warranted. And we've often backed up agents agreeing to contribute toward resolving issues that, say, come up at walkthroughs (which are obviously not our responsibility) to keep a client happy and ensure that a deal closes. You need rules, but you also need to know when to relax them.

9. Resilience. For years, I've been asking audiences to share their favorite "great service" story with me, and I've noticed a familiar pattern. Most of those stories involve a "recovery" from a bad situation. That is, the customer was unhappy, made a complaint, and the company then went above and beyond to fix the situation. Essentially, the company took a bad experience and used it as an opportunity to create a great one.

Why do those stories come up again and again? I think it's because there's something distinctly memorable about a "recovery," maybe the sharp shift in emotion that you feel when a situation morphs from intolerable to delightful. I can remember when my brother was supposed to have a room at the Hilton San Francisco for the annual Inman Connect conference, but his reservation got screwed up. And, of course, the hotel was now fully booked. He could have been out of luck, or, even worse, been forced to stay with me! But the manager intervened and gave him the only room available: a Presidential Suite. So while I was hunkered down in a typically cramped 200-square foot urban hotel room, he spent the week in a two-story palace with a fireplace, a wet bar, and a grand piano. I didn't even get to stay in the room, and I still remember the story. Why? Because it was a brilliant recovery.

Every agent is capable of the recovery. No matter how good you are, you're going to mess something up sometimes. That's okay. That happens. The question is what you do next. Do you shrink from the problem or do you take on the challenge and use it as an opportunity to do something special?

RESILIENCE

Believe me, you can turn any situation around. I once had to sue a client for stiffing us on a commission, took him all the way to trial and judgment and collected almost $50,000. It was a stressful situation, but throughout the entire trial I treated him with respect and consideration, essentially taking on the demeanor that "I hate to do this, but I have to stick up for my agent." And after we won, when he pleaded with me to give him a discount on the judgment, even after forcing us to go through that whole judicial process, I still shaved it a little for him to avoid having to deal with an appeal.

Two years later, I heard my name called in a parking lot, and saw him running up to me. I honestly thought he was going to hit me and was bracing myself for ~~fighting back~~ taking a beating. Instead, he shook my hand and told me how happy he was to see me, because he had a friend selling a house and wanted me to hook him up with an agent. The guy I sued gave me a referral! Why? Because even in a difficult circumstance, what he took out of that whole experience is that I treated him with respect and consideration. Essentially, he had such a terrible service experience with my company that he only paid us when we got a judgment against him, but we were still able to eventually recover. That's resilience.

10. **Delight.** I can remember when the iPhone first came out with Siri, the voice assistant. A friend got one, and a bunch of us gathered around it asking silly questions just to see what Siri would say.

"Siri, what are you wearing?"

"Aluminosilicate glass and stainless steel. Nice, huh?"

"Siri, I love you."

"Oh, I bet you say that to all your Apple products."

"Siri, am I fat?"

"I would prefer not to say."

And so on. We spent about an hour just having fun talking to a phone. Not *on* the phone, *to* the phone. And it occurred to me that many months before, a bunch of Apple engineers had taken the time to program clever or funny responses to probably hundreds or thousands of stupid questions like those, for no practical reason. Just to entertain.

That's "delight," the feeling of enchantment that you sometimes get from an amazing client service experience, almost like the way you feel when you see a magic trick you can't figure out. Apple isn't the only tech company that works to create these kinds of "Easter Eggs," hidden tricks in a product designed simply to delight the user. If you have an Amazon Echo, ask "Alexa, can you sing?" and see what happens. And make sure to Google something on your birthday, so you can see the special display you get on the home page.

But "delight" is not limited to technology companies. For example, Danny Meyer, in his wonderful book *Setting the Table*, explained how his restaurants always make it a practice to ask whether a reservation is being made for a special occasion, like a birthday or anniversary. Why? Because it allows the host or hostess to congratulate the diners when they arrive with a "Happy Birthday" or "Happy Anniversary." It's a delightful trick, because people make those reservations months in advance, and never remember being asked about the special occasion, so they can't figure out how the restaurant knew. It's like magic.

DELIGHT

The thing about "delight" is that it's supposed to be sort of "frivolous." No one buys an iPhone to ask Siri silly questions or eats at the Union Square Cafe because they congratulate you on your anniversary. Rather, "delight" is a bonus, something that you create naturally when you're fully committed to providing an outstanding client service.

For example, I know an agent who does professional photography on every listing for her marketing, which is a great service for clients. She doesn't do it just for her high-end listings, she does it for every listing, no matter the price point. And she uploads those photos into Shutterfly to make a coffee table book that she gives to the clients at the closing, as a keepsake so that they can remember this house that they lived in. Her clients love it. And they love her, not because of the photobook itself but because the book is simply one manifestation of the myriad of other ways she delivered a thoughtful, outstanding client experience.

Similarly, if you're truly committed to delivering a great experience to your clients, you'll find those opportunities to add a little bit of magic along the way.

Bringing the WOW!

I call this kind of delight "Bringing the Wow!"—a magical experience where you absolutely blow a client away with the service you provide to them. It's more than just a great service experience, it's where your attention to your client's needs creates an unexpectedly authentic, moving moment.

Indeed, you can't really predict when you're going to bring the "Wow!" because it's not just about you and the service you're providing. It's about the client, and her specific needs that you might not even be fully aware of. And it's about timing. You almost have to get lucky, with your service hitting the client at just the right moment in just the right way to create the magical "Wow!"

For example, I told the story at the beginning of the book about Bill, who dropped off a bag of rock salt to all his best referral clients. I'm sure all of them appreciated it, but he created an unforgettable "Wow!" when one of his clients got that rock salt at just the right moment in his life.

But as baseball player Branch Rickey once famously said, "Luck is the residue of design." You only get that opportunity to "Bring the Wow!" when you're constantly thinking expansively and creatively of ways to make people happy. You keep doing the little things right, and occasionally, your little thing turns into a big thing. You hit single after single after single and then, suddenly, you hit a home run. Bill delivered hundreds of bags of rock salt to his appreciative clients over the years, efforts that gave him that singular opportunity to create a magical experience when he was in the right place at the right time.

In other words, if you're always doing really nice things for people, you're giving yourself the opportunity to create that special "Wow!" experience. Danny Meyer tells a story in his book, for example, about a couple who came to one of his restaurants on their anniversary. A few minutes after sitting down, the husband called over the maître d' to ask a question. It seemed he had purchased a very expensive bottle of champagne to celebrate when they got back home. He had forgotten to chill it, though, so he had put it in the freezer as they left so it would be cold when they returned. Now, he was starting to get concerned that he might have made a mistake.

Unfortunately, as the maître d' explained, the champagne would, in fact, explode. Ugh! That's not what the husband wanted to hear. He stood up, explaining to his wife that he would have to go home and pull the bottle out of the freezer, interrupting their night out.

But the maître d' stopped him, saying that if the couple was okay giving him their address, he would go himself and take the champagne out of the freezer. They happily agreed, the maître d' took a cab over, moved the bottle to the refrigerator, and then went back to the restaurant to reassure them that everything was okay.

And later, when that couple got home to pop that rescued bottle of champagne, they found it wasn't alone. It was sitting next to some dessert chocolates, a small tin of caviar, and a note from the maître d' congratulating them on their anniversary.

That's a "Wow!"

Those kinds of experiences don't just happen. They're the residue of a creative and expansive commitment to providing exceptional service experiences for other people. If your entire orientation is toward thinking about what people need, and how to give it to them, you invariably find opportunities to "Bring the Wow!"

Part Three Conclusion: Be Great at Your Job

My first job out of law school was clerking for a federal appellate judge. It was fascinating work: reviewing briefs, writing memos, helping him prepare for oral arguments, and writing the first drafts of his opinions.

Over the course of helping him prepare for about 500 different cases, I realized something interesting: most of the time, the quality of the attorneys representing the parties didn't matter. Why? Because the facts were the facts, and the law was the law. Even a miserable attorney was likely to win with the facts and law on his side. And even Clarence Darrow himself was not going to prevail if he had a loser of a case. Most of the cases I reviewed were like that.

Once in a while, though, the quality of the lawyering made a difference. The lawyer found a point of law lesser attorneys would have missed, or she made a persuasive oral argument, or wrote a compelling brief with a message that resonated with the court. And she won where a lesser attorney would have lost. Not all the time. Not even most of the time. Maybe 10% of the time.

I think most professional situations are like that. People don't always need the best attorney to represent them—even an okay lawyer will be fine—because their case is pretty straightforward, and they have the facts and law on their side. They don't necessarily need the best doctor, because their diagnosis is pretty obvious, and the treatment is standard. They don't need the best electrician, because pretty much any competent professional can fix their wiring. Most of the time, they don't need someone great, they just need someone competent.

But if you had a really high-stakes lawsuit, or a virulent disease, or a serious electrical failure, do you want to take that chance? Do you want to get someone merely competent, hoping that you're one of the 90%? Or do you want the best lawyer, and the best doctor, and the best electrician—just in case you're one of the 10%?

The answer is obvious. You never want to settle for someone merely competent, at least not for anything important, because you never know if you're in that 10% of cases where a great professional can make a difference.

Real estate's the same way. Even a mediocre real estate agent can sell most listings. Indeed, you'd probably agree that most of the homes in your market are in fact sold by mediocre real estate agents! And some of those listings are sold by agents who are downright terrible at their jobs.

But some of those homes listed by mediocre-or-worse agents don't sell, do they? Or some of them sell, but at a lower price than they should have. Or they sold, but they took longer to sell than other similar homes.

The same is true for buyers. We only see the transactions for the buyers who actually managed to close. What about the buyers who weren't able to close, because their agent wasn't strong enough to read their needs, find them the right home, negotiate a good deal, or shepherd them through the transactional minefield?

That's the calculation that real estate consumers need to make. They don't know whether their home sale or purchase is one of the 90% that pretty much any agent can handle, or one of the 10% that only a great agent can close. But they shouldn't take their chances, should they? Why hire a mediocre agent when you can generally get a great agent for around the same price?

Unfortunately, too many clients aren't choosy enough about their real estate agents. They're willing to take the up-person, the one who responds to their email inquiry, the host at the most recent open house they went to, without even thinking about whether that agent is any good at her job.

Indeed, we've built most of our traditional lead generation infrastructure around the idea that potential clients aren't that choosy. Up-time, "find out more" website buttons, open houses, cold calling—almost all of our prospecting methodologies depend on clients simply accepting the agent who reaches out or responds to them. Most clients don't choose their agent; their agent chooses them.

We've even fostered this impression by the way we market, or fail to market, ourselves. People think that all agents are the same partly because the industry aggressively levels the playing field, never differentiating agents by their expertise in our consumer marketing. Brokers and franchise systems won't do it because they don't want to alienate their middle- or low-producing agents by encouraging consumers to choose agents based on track record and merit. NAR won't do it because they can't promote top agents over the bulk of their membership. Indeed, NAR's basic pitch is that as long as consumers select a REALTOR, they're fine. But virtually every agent in the country is a REALTOR. Are they *all* going to give those consumers the same great experience?

As an industry, we should want consumers to work with the best agents, rather than protect the middling ones. But we don't. And so we feed that misperception that we're all the same.

Now, things are mostly changing for the better, as consumers become more selective about their real estate agent and broker. They're reading the reviews, and checking ratings, and even sometimes evaluating performance stats. We're slowly moving in the direction where clients become choosy and will increasingly be rewarding the agents who are great at their jobs.

We have to encourage that trend. Agent by agent, broker by broker, we need to transform the perception of our industry. We have to show, by everything that we do, that great real estate agents make a difference. They get more deals done. They get better terms. They give clients a better experience. And they're the ones who can handle those tough cases, those borderline cases, those 10% of cases where a great agent is the difference between success and failure.

And that starts with you and the work you do.

It starts with being great at the job of managing your clients, the job of giving them an amazing transactional experience.

So be great.

Conclusion

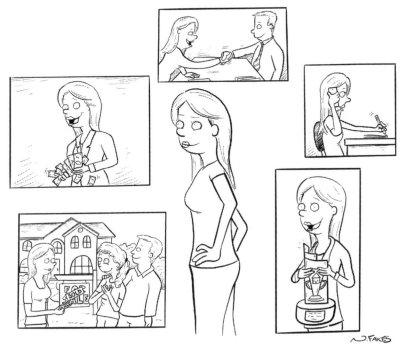

If you're great at your job, all sorts of
good things happen for you.

Be Great at Your Job

BE GREAT AT YOUR JOB.

Be great at your job of helping people sell homes.

Be great at your job of helping people buy homes.

Be great at your job of helping people even when they're not buying or selling homes.

Just be great at your job, every part of your job, from developing clients, to converting clients, to managing clients:

Client Development. If you're great at your job, you're great at expanding your conception of who your clients are, recognizing that everyone, even if they're not buying or selling right now, needs a real estate agent. So you're great at providing that Sphere of Support with the CORE Courtesy Services, reaching out to them with information about the market, their home, and the community, and encouraging them to come to you whenever they have real estate questions. You're also great at providing the Top 100 people in that Sphere with an even higher level of intimate service, to cultivate them into a reliable referral base. And you're great at providing services to anyone you come across in your client development work, from the neighbors of your new listings to that FSBO seller down the block, as a means of building the kind of relationship that kindles lead generation.

Client Conversion. If you're great at your job, you're great at counseling your clients in that initial listing or buyer meeting, focusing on their needs rather than their own. You're great at listening to them so that you can identify what they need from you, and how you can give it to them. You're great at articulating your modern value proposition, rather than relying on the antiquated notion of real estate agent as gatekeeper. And you're great at taking a collaborative client-oriented approach to pricing, guiding your clients through the process rather than simply telling them what they should do.

Client Management. If you're great at your job, you're great at providing your buyers and sellers with a delightful client experience. You recognize that your clients need more than just a closed deal, and even more than simply acceptable terms—they need an outstanding experience from consultation to contract to closing. So you're great at taking a "Clean Windows" approach to your business, eliminating the very possibility of problems. You're great at implementing those standards through Action Plans that create consistency in your execution. And you live the 10 Elements of a Great Client Experience to create delight in your clients.

In other words, be great at everything you do in your business. Every interaction you have with anyone is an opportunity to think expansively about what they need, creatively about how to give it to them, and execute well. It's not just about your active buyers and listed sellers. It's everyone. What does that florist at the cocktail party need? How about that guy selling his house on his own? Or the couple who just brought you in to talk about listing their house?

They're all clients. You're their agent. Take care of them. And be great at the job of taking care of them.

Not because it's better for your clients.

Although it is.

And not because it's better for your industry.

Although it is.

But because it's better for you.

That's how you can be successful in this business. That's how you make money. That's how you build a better life. If you're great at your job, all sorts of good things will happen for you:

- *You'll close deals.* If you're great at marketing, pricing, and staging your listings, you'll sell more of them. If you're great at establishing a rapport with your buyers, you'll keep them loyal to you, discern their preferences, and find them the right home. If you're great at holding your deals together, at managing your client through the difficult pitfalls of the transaction, you'll be more likely to close them. And that's how you become successful: by actually closing deals. In contrast, if you're not that good at your job, your listings sit on the market, your buyers flake on you, and your deals fall apart. You're not going to make a lot of money that way.

- *You'll build a reputation.* If you're great at your job, you'll earn the kind of reputation that compels people to seek you out. You'll foster a general sense in the community that you're a great agent, someone who provides clients with an amazing experience and outstanding results. Think about it this way—you probably know who the best attorneys in your area are, without remembering who exactly referred you to them. You just picked up on their general reputation. Well, you can generate that same viral word-of-mouth.

- *You'll get more referrals.* If you're great at your job, you generate happy clients. Satisfied clients say nice things about you to their friends. Those friends sometimes need to buy or sell a home. Voilà! You've just gotten a new deal simply because you did a great job. I'm actually amazed at how many "referral generating systems" you can buy at conventions that tell you that you're going to get referrals because you send people seeds in the mail or a hokey newsletter but say nothing about the importance of being great at your job. Believe me, if you don't do a great job for your clients, it doesn't matter how many refrigerator magnets you send them. If you burn your clients, they'll burn you.

- *You'll gain confidence.* If you're great at your job, you'll be confident about doing the business development you need to generate new clients and opportunities. When you're good at something, you want to do more of it. So it's a lot easier to call that unrepresented seller when you absolutely know you can do a better job selling her house than she can. And you'll be a lot more comfortable at your listing consultations if you can fearlessly pull out your tablet to show that seller how well you marketed your last home.

- *You'll get a marketing differentiator.* If you're great at your job, you'll be able to stand out from the other agents in the business—in a good way! Beautiful photos and collateral show that you're great at marketing your listings. Glowing reviews, real testimonials, and personalized reference letters show that you keep your clients happy. Analytics demonstrate that you sell your homes more quickly and for closer to the asking price than other agents.

Those are all marketing differentiators in an industry where too many agents are just "they're all the same" commodities.

- *You'll command better fees.* If you're great at your job, you'll protect yourself from discounters. You'll be confident enough in your abilities to command a reasonable fee, and you'll get better results that will justify charging more than some numbskull working out of his basement. Basically, you'll be able to answer the question, "why should we hire you if this other broker will charge us less?" honestly and convincingly.

Most importantly, you'll have a happier life. Because you know what happens as you expand your conception of what your clients need? You start expanding your conception of what *everyone* needs. Not just your buyers and sellers, or the people in your Sphere, or the potential clients that you're trying to develop through your lead generation. Everyone.

Why? Because you can't turn it off. You spend all day thinking expansively about what people need, and creatively about how you can take care of them, and you can't just shut it down when the whistle blows. Invariably, you start broadening your perspective of what everyone needs. You become someone who thinks about other people's needs before your own. And that's a good thing, not just for your business, but for you.

Since I started following the CORE philosophy as part of my work, it's changed my life. I'm a better husband, a better father, a better friend, a better citizen. My whole orientation has changed to look, almost instinctively and reflexively, for ways to service the needs of other people. I'm a better person, and a happier person, because of that.

Think expansively about what people need. Think creatively about how to take care of them. And then execute well. You'll be a better real estate agent and a more successful real estate agent. More importantly, you'll be a better, and happier, person.

Be great at your job. Because if you're great at your job, all sorts of good things happen to you.

Afterword:
Where Do We Go From Here?

I'M DONE.

Now, it's your turn.

When I sat down to write this book, I consciously framed it as an articulation of the CORE Formula:

First, think expansively about what real estate agents need. For years, the real estate training industry has focused obsessively on unrelenting and tireless lead generation as the key to real estate agent success. But as a broker, and a trainer, I saw a massive chasm between what the training industry taught and how the top agents in my market acted. The most successful agents in my market were not tireless prospectors. They didn't spend all their time on the phones cold calling, or all their money sending mailings to their farm. Instead, they spent their time doing great work for their clients, getting their listings sold, finding their buyers homes, closing their deals, building their reputation. They were great at their jobs.

So I thought about what real estate agents like you needed. You certainly didn't need another training manual reiterating conventional wisdom, hoary scripts, and empty promises that you can be successful if you'll just cold call for three hours a day. You can find plenty of those. Rather, you needed a guide to show you how to become successful by doing better work for your clients.

Second, think creatively about how to service that need. Over the years of watching successful agents, and then trying to distill what I learned so I could teach it to others, I gradually developed an approach for building a prosperous real estate business: Client-Oriented Real Estate ("CORE"). I realized that the key to success was to focus on the long-term goal of making clients happy, rather than the short-term desire for an active lead. So I slowly built a program around taking an expansive view of what clients need and a creative perspective on how to give it to them, focusing on the major inflection points of the business—lead generation, listing presentations, and client service—and taking a client-oriented approach to all of them.

I realized that it all tied together holistically: if you were great at one aspect of your job, it was easier to do other parts of your job. For example, being great at marketing your listings not only helped get your client's home sold, but also helped you in your next listing consultation, when you could point to that beautiful marketing as an exemplar of the quality of the work you did. And it also helped you in your client development, because beautiful marketing generates more leads and gives you a reason to approach those expired sellers with the message that you will do things differently.

Over time, often through trial-and-error, and with help from an immensely patient group of wonderful real estate agents, I figured out what worked and what didn't. So I was able to write a prescription for being great at your job that was based on actual agent experiences, not just some theories that I developed in a lab. Everything in this book is practical, actionable, and proven.

Third, execute well. This is where you come in. The book is done. You just read it, or skimmed it, or maybe skipped to here to see how it ends. For better or worse, the concepts are all here, the ideas are all explained. But that's not enough to ensure that you can become a great real estate agent. The rest is up to you, and how you execute on these ideas. Because execution matters.

So how do you execute on these concepts? Here are a couple of suggestions:

1. *Work with a good broker.* It helps if you have a good broker, someone whose values are aligned with the client-oriented spirit of this book. After all, how are you supposed to provide amazing client experiences for your clients if your broker doesn't provide the support that you (and your clients) need? If you choose your broker based entirely on split, rather than the quality of the work that they can do for you, then you're making the mistake that too many consumers make, thinking that "they're all the same," and that a good broker can't make a difference. Now, this isn't to say that high-split brokers cannot provide quality services to agents and clients. Certainly they can. I've

seen good transactional fee brokers who provide amazing services as part of their package. But too many agents get seduced into choosing a broker based on price rather than value. Instead, find a broker who provides both value and values.

2. *Get a coach.* I'm a big believer in coaching and have seen it work for a variety of agents. All good coaches provide the single most important tool you need: accountability. They'll help you set goals, make commitments to those goals, and then hold you accountable for sticking to those commitments. And, if they're good at what they do, they'll inspire you to work harder and get better.

Which coach? I can't make a recommendation without knowing you and your own strengths and weaknesses. At different times in my own life, I've been inspired by icons like Mike Ferry, Floyd Wickman, Tom Ferry, Brian Buffini, and Mike Staver. And I know agents and brokers who have had career-changing experiences with educators and coaches as diverse as Dan Smith, Bryon Ellington, Leigh Brown, Larry Kendall, Steve Harney, Verl Workman, Travis Robertson, Jared James, David Knox, Candy Miles-Crocker, Amy Chorew, Sean Carpenter, Darryl Davis, Dirk Zeller, Martha Webb, Matthew Ferrara, Michael LaFido, Tim and Julie Harris, Bernice Ross, Katie Lance, Jeff Lobb, Mark Leader, and Alyssa Hellman—and I'm sure a bunch of other wonderful people that I'm forgetting as I write this.

Now, most of these coaches have their own programs, their own approaches, but I generally feel as if the CORE program is consistent with any coaching course that isn't based on treating clients like marks in a three-card monte game. Find a coach who aligns with the way you want to run your business and live your life. If you wish to embrace the CORE philosophy, talk to the coach about it. They might be willing to adapt their own program to your needs. And if they don't know what you're talking about, encourage them to buy a copy of this book. Or, even better, buy many, many copies.

Now, people who have read drafts of this book have asked me why I don't provide coaching myself to help people execute on the CORE principles. Good question! The answer is that I already have a job. Along with my brothers, and my mother, I run a real estate company with over 1,200 agents, all of whom deserve my full attention. More or less, to one degree or another, I coach all of them.

But I recognize that, sadly, not everyone who reads this book can come work with my company. So here's what the rest of you can do...

3. *Go to www.joerand.com.* At our website, we're going to be providing supplemental material to help anyone who wants to incorporate the CORE philosophy in their life. If you go to our site, you'll find examples of Project Plans that set out checklists for common agent tasks, Courtesy Package materials, marketing pieces that articulate a client-oriented sensibility, and other resources. You'll also find my blog, which I might actually start writing again now that this book is done, and links to my social media profiles and pages.

More importantly, I'm going to be releasing a "Practice Guide" with practical step-by-step instructions for executing the CORE concepts from this book. I framed *How to be a Great Real Estate Agent* as an overview of the CORE philosophy, to help you adopt a client-oriented mindset. I didn't want to get all bogged down in the weeds with detailed instructions about how to execute on these ideas. So we're going to be publishing that Practice Guide at www.joerand.com as a reference for agents who want to incorporate the CORE philosophy into their business.

Eventually, you will also find a range of educational resources that I'll start working on as soon as I finish the next six paragraphs, including continuing education courses dedicated to teaching the CORE Services. If you'd like to help get these courses approved in your state, reach out to me through the site.

Finally, you can also come see me speak! I have started taking more speaking opportunities since the publication of *Disruptors, Discounters, and Doubters*, visiting individual brokerages, state associations, and national conferences. Check out my schedule at www.joerand.com, and if you'd like to look into booking me for an event, reach out to me through the site. You can also sign up for my mailing list that will keep you updated on my appearances, new resources at the site, blog posts, and even plans for the next book!

Acknowledgements

THIS BOOK REPRESENTS THE CULMINATION OF YEARS OF work with the great agents and employees at the Rand organization, and I can't thank them enough for allowing me to learn from them. They represent the best of what this industry has to offer, and it has been my honor to work with them. If you found ideas you liked in the book, they almost certainly bubbled up from the agents I worked with over the years. All the bad ideas you didn't like? Those were totally my own.

I also want to thank my partners (who also happen to be family members): Marsha, Greg, Matt, and Dan Rand, who had the patience and generosity to allow me to write when I should have been, you know, working. They are the best partners I could ever have asked for.

And I need to thank the people who helped me put together this book: Julie Trelstad for her wise counsel throughout the process, Alexandra Battey for her tireless work on the manuscript, and Nate Fakes for his cleverness in translating my dumb ideas into fun illustrations. My thanks to my friend George Pejoves, who took the cover photo and did the best he could with the raw material I gave him. And although you're reading this, not listening to it, I also want to thank Kevin Thomsen for producing and Greg Talenfeld for engineering the production of the audiobook.

Also, I should thank some friends and colleagues who gave me such helpful and encouraging feedback on earlier drafts of the book. That includes my friend Dan Smith, author of *Failing Greatly* (the next book you should read!); Esther Berkowitz, who did meticulous work proofreading the final manuscript; and the Rand Realty agents and managers who made up the "Free Lunch For Reading My New Book Crew"—Kim Meade, JP Endres, Jean Tickell, Debra Pfeffer,

Laurel Lustgarten, Victor Polce, and Joe Goetchius. The book is better for their efforts.

Finally, I want to thank my wife Linie, a real estate agent and manager herself, who has been my sounding board for every good, bad, or mediocre idea I've had over the past 20 years. She saved all of you from some terrible, terrible mistakes. More importantly, every day, she inspires me to be a better person.

And, of course, I want to acknowledge my kids Jake and Relly, who did absolutely nothing to help me write this book, but who, nevertheless, make it all worthwhile.

Thanks, everyone. Let's go be great.

J.R.
Nyack, New York
January 2019